D0921961

COMEDY OF VANITY & LIFE-TERMS

COMEDY OF VANITY
&
LIFE-TERMS

ELIAS CANETTI

Introduction by Klaus Völker

Translation by Gitta Honegger

PERFORMING ARTS JOURNAL PUBLICATIONS
NEW YORK CITY

Library of Congress Cataloging in Publication Data
Comedy of Vanity & Life-Terms
Library of Congress Catalog Card No.: 82-62100
ISBN: 0-933826-30-3 (cloth)
ISBN: 0-933826-31-1 (paper)

Design: Gautam Dasgupta
Printed in the United States of America

Publication of this book has been made possible in part by a grant from the National Endowment for the Arts, Washington, D.C., a federal agency, and public funds received from the New York State Council on the Arts.

PAJ Playscripts/General Editors:
Bonnie Marranca and Gautam Dasgupta

Contents

Translator's Note

Canetti's concept of "acoustic masks," which Klaus Völker describes in his introduction, applies only to *Comedy of Vanity*. This play presents great problems for a translator because it is written in strong Viennese dialect whose different "acoustic masks" represent the many varieties of Viennese German. Each character's particular use of syntax, pronunciation and choice of vocabulary reveals his class, social ambitions, and the personal (linguistic) strategies he uses to achieve his goals. Acoustic masks are very specific. They are ethnic and deeply rooted in local culture and mentality.

Any translation can only be an approximation, an indication of the original relationship between language and culture. To adapt the text to a specifically American environment would be wrong since the characters' behavior is conditioned by a class system which is a carry-over from the hierarchy of the Habsburg monarchy and its standards of status and culture. So, the abuse of language by the nouveau riche, the social climbers, would-be academics on the one hand, and the have-nots and outcasts on the other, is in imitation of or a reaction to the elite which always (rightly or wrongly) considers itself a cultural elite as well. Canetti, like Karl Kraus, Ödön von Horváth, and Johann Nestroy sets his traps and locates his satirical attacks inside a language that betrays itself not by *what* but by *how* something is said or covered up. Everything becomes a matter of style, and the lack of it betrays itself precisely in its various (linguistic) disguises.

Replacing the different Viennese accents and dialects with American dialects does not solve the translation problem since their social and cultural origins, their reasons for being, are different. Canetti's very special social satire would miss its target completely in the politics and strategies of the English language.

To the Anglo-Saxon ear, much of the preoccupation with linguistic strategies, posing and game-playing seems wordy, flowery, indulgent. Without cutting any passages I have tried to tighten up and focus the language according to American patterns of speech, which resulted in the inevitable loss of some of the original resonances and colors. However, these elements can be brought back onto the stage nonverbally through the *comic gestus* of the individual characters and the production itself. The theatricality of the American vaudeville tradition seems a particularly adaptable frame for the staging of the play as a universal parable about mass hysteria.

G. H.

THE PLAYS OF ELIAS CANETTI

Klaus Völker

*The profession of the contemporary playwright begins with oppos-
ing the theatre as it is today, and must not be permitted to continue.*

Elias Canetti

Elias Canetti was born in 1905 in Rustshuk, Bulgaria. He attended elemen-
tary and high schools in Manchester, Vienna, Zurich and Frankfurt, and
received a Ph.D. in Chemistry from the University of Vienna in 1929. His
first novel *Auto-da-Fé* was published in 1935 without attracting much attention.
However, he found some very important readers who recognized his achieve-
ment, most importantly Hermann Broch, Alban Berg and the painter Alfred
Kubin. Thomas Mann also congratulated the "daring young writer, who
shuns neither terror nor humor."

At the time *Auto-da-Fé* was published, Canetti had already written two
plays, *The Wedding* (1932) and *Comedy of Vanity* (1933/34). These were daring
plays in their treatment of structure, style, and language, which explains why
they were not produced when they were written. Austria's theatrical establishment, with its emphasis on naturalistic acting, was unsuited to those plays,
and the various progressive "fringe" groups existing at that time were
primarily presenting anti-fascist agit-prop theatre. When some of these groups
became interested finally in Canetti's plays, it was too late. In March 1938 the
Nazis marched into Austria.

Canetti emigrated to London, where he still lives, dividing his time between
London and Zurich. His major social-anthropological work, *Crowds and Power*,
was written in exile, its first part appearing in Germany in 1960. It was not

until *Auto-da-Fé* was published again, in 1963, that Canetti found a larger readership. New books appeared: *The Human Province, Ear Witness, Voices of Marrakesh* and *The Conscience of Words*. Two autobiographical works, *The Tongue Set Free* and *The Torch in My Ear* contributed to his rising popularity and fame. Only now was he recognized as a German language writer equal to Hermann Broch, Robert Musil and Robert Walser. During the last few years he has been awarded many distinguished literary prizes, among them the Georg Büchner Award, the Franz Kafka Award and, finally, the 1981 Nobel Prize for Literature.

Canetti's plays are the least known work of his oeuvre. Partly because of the inhospitable conditions in the theatre at that time and partly because Karl Kraus had such difficulty in his attempts to stage the works of Johann Nestroy and Jacques Offenbach, Canetti decided to become his own interpreter and he began to hold public readings of his plays. To this day he remains an ideal performer of his plays, although they have been successfully produced in the meantime, thanks to Austrian director Hans Hollmann who has staged the most significant productions of *Comedy of Vanity* in Basel in 1977, and in Vienna in 1979. In 1983 he plans to direct *Life-Terms* in Stuttgart and *The Wedding* in Munich. Canetti's brilliant presentation of his own work is the most convincing argument against those critics and theatre people who claim that his plays are literature, not theatre. Canetti doesn't just read them, he communicates their structure and musicality. He is an accomplished performer in showing each character's "acoustic mask." In creating his characters Canetti himself works as an "ear witness": there is no stronger dramatic material than people's speech habits and patterns. Like Karl Kraus, he conceives and employs language as the "great traitor" of human character.

Canetti considers what he calls "acoustic masks" the most important element of dramatic construction. They are a person's language reservoir, his favorite words and phrases, his use of language and the manner of speaking by which he presents or betrays himself. His language gives him a distinct shape that sets him off against his surroundings, makes him completely different from everyone else, just as his physiognomy is unique. "The acoustic shape of a person, the constant elements in his speech, this language which originated in and simultaneously with him, which is his alone and will disappear with him, this is what I call his 'acoustic mask' '' is Canetti's own description of the concept.

His plays are developed around one central "idea"; they have no plot, no linear development in any conventional sense. This idea, however, is played out in many variations which lead up to the dramatic climax. This is less the case in his third play *Life-Terms,* which was written in 1952 and produced in 1956 at the Oxford Playhouse Company in England. Here the basic idea is introduced as an abstract concept, without the characters acquiring a specific physiognomy through their individual use of language.

The Wedding is Canetti's first and most frequently produced play, whose first performance in Braunschweig in 1965 was followed by productions in Stockholm, Zurich, Cologne, Berlin, Bonn and on German television. It features an apartment building and the people who own it, constructed it, take care of it, live in it or want to gain possession of it. All aspects of the building surface in the relationships of the people whose thoughts and actions focus exclusively on the house. The characters' greed also shapes their sexual interests and behavior. The actual wedding party transforms into macabre coupling games until the whole building collapses at the height of pleasures which nobody enjoys. These figures in a dance of death are creatures of a decaying social order, the ugly philistines and monsters of George Grosz, whose drawings inspired the writing of *The Wedding*. This collapse is a prophetic metaphor for actual historical collapse a few years later.

The plays of Canetti belong to the Viennese tradition of satire which includes Kraus and Ödön von Horváth. Canetti is an analytical playwright who makes fools out of bourgeois society in order to expose the abyss underneath its blatant stupidities, as Nestroy did before him. In literature aimed at unveiling and exposing, the mirror is a firmly established convention. It exposes truth, and serves as a window to the real world in the act of stripping down illusions. Some people revel in their mirror-image, others are afraid of it. Raimund's misanthrope Rappelkopf (in *Der Alpenkönig und der Menschefeind*) curses the mirror as the "seducer of the whole world" and smashes it to pieces. Herr von Lips in Nestroy's *Der Zerrissene* admits to his vanity in front of the mirror, but as soon as he reveals the truth about himself and the world he masks it in a fit of laughter.

The starting point for *Comedy of Vanity,* Canetti's second play, is a new law against vanity, which calls for the immediate destruction of all mirrors, photographs and films. The government hopes this will eliminate vanity once and for all. The immediate effect is mass hysteria which drives everyone to destroy their pictures and mirrors in a frenzy. With their pictures, people sacrifice their last remnants of human substance. Barrass, the packer, carries a bale of pictures to throw into a huge fire. Oppressed up to now, he is suddenly permitted to exercise power, to become a superman. "I'll smash the whole city if I goddam please." Shakee, the teacher, who had a stammer, is able to speak with self-confident fluency whenever he announces the official regulations. Even babies are swept along by the fanaticism of the crowds who rush to the fire to burn their photographs. Kaldaun Jr. screams in his carriage full of joy: "Fy-ah! Fy-ah!"

The second part of the play shows life without mirrors. People spy on and denounce each other. Mirrors flourish in the black market. Some obey the orders with obsessive persistency, others conform rather timidly. Everybody, however, is ready secretly to transgress the law. The "mirror," which Tristan Tzara calls "the fruit of all fears" has been repressed but it controls the actions and reactions of the characters.

The play's third part takes place in the glaring light of a large hall of mirrors, where everyone can secretly satisfy his vanity for good money. "Each mirror has a person sitting in front of it, motionless, hands on hips, sharp elbows pointed aggressively toward the neighbor on the other side. No one is talking. No one is breathing." It seems the group is gathered in perfect harmony. No one knows who is seated next to him. "Everyone would be scared to death of his neighbor, but elbows are blind, and those moments cost a lot of money." A chance accident disrupts the order and confronts the people with the artificiality of their situation. They revolt. Everyone grabs his mirror and runs out.

In Canetti's play Nestroy's ambiguous laughter at human vanity becomes an apocalyptic grotesquery. Vanity, whether repressed or exaggerated, is always ridiculous and dangerous. The play, whose actual antagonist is the crowd, begins with the barker's mesmerizing "And we, and we, and we . . ." which organizes the collective frenzy, and ends with a catastrophic mass revolt against the new order to hysteria, shouts of "I," "I," "I." The intoxication with freedom in a crowd manipulated by a totalitarian order is not a popular revolt, but rather an impotent demonstration of destroyed self-awareness.

Comedy of Vanity was written for the most part in 1933, after the Nazis came to power in Germany. The book burning was the concrete historical background of the play, which starts with the smashing of mirrors. Completed in 1934, the play was published in German for the first time in 1950. Both *The Wedding* and *Comedy of Vanity* premiered in Braunschweig, Germany, in 1965. The director of the first production made the grave mistake of setting *Comedy of Vanity* in the context of the Third Reich. In contrast to the play, which calls for a total prohibition of all pictures and photographs, the stage was plastered with Hitler photographs, and slides were used constantly to supply the play with documentary material it doesn't need. Like Karl Kraus's *The Last Days of Mankind*, *Comedy of Vanity* is constructed entirely from quotes, or rather voices and sounds, collected by Canetti, the "ear witness," who, unlike Kraus, was able to transpose his documentary material into a perfect dramatic structure. (How much *Comedy of Vanity* was influenced by Kraus is evident in its first draft which, like *The Last Days of Mankind*, features the characters of Grumbler and Optimist, who comment on the events of the play.)

World War II lies between Canetti's early plays and *Life-Terms*. During the war Canetti chose to move away from purely literary efforts, turning instead to scientific research to further expand his philosophy of the crowd. "Now it was no longer possible, not even for a brief moment, to distance or disguise oneself. Only those who were serious in their effort to comprehend had the right to any form of life." His *Crowds and Power* was an attempt to search in early myths and the history of insanity for the truth about power and the origin of crowds. *Life-Terms* shows the lessons and experiences Canetti gained from investigating the phenomenon of crowds and power. The power of the "survivor," according to him, is not dangerous as long as he makes it the most demanding task of his life "not to get used to death." Life must never be permitted to distinguish itself solely as something leading to death.

Life-Terms takes place in a society where everyone knows the moment of his death. At birth everyone has placed around his neck a locket which contains the date of birth and date of death. People's names refer to the number of years they have to live. There is no more uncertainty about death, nobody can be killed or die a natural death before his "moment." The only crime is telling one's day of death. It is permitted to know the number of years a person has to live, but not the year of birth. Everyone is predictable, a person's only value is his age. People with a high life expectancy belong to the privileged class, the rest are treated with condescension and derision. In this society the so-called locketeer is in charge of upholding the law. He is also the official who claims the locket at the time of death.

There are a few "fools" who prefer the deathly uncertainty of earlier times to the new tranquility which doesn't permit any freedom. Fifty, a skeptic, eventually discovers that the lockets are empty, everything is as uncertain as it has always been. Consequently, he opens the door to chaos. Now that the burden of individual responsibility has suddenly become greater, no one is able to deal with the newly gained freedom. It is a freedom that leads to death, nonetheless. Everyone is afraid.

In this play Canetti shows to what degree people are susceptible to totalitarian power if they accept death without protest and let it control their lives. To accept death means to deny oneself any possibility of transformation and change. The alternative to death is not eternal life but rather a better, more meaningful life, which has been liberated from the domination of death.

Fifty proves that the entire control mechanism hinges on the "moment" of death, which has been elevated to a taboo. He recants his knowledge for strategic purposes in order to gain extra time. But the final truth is that people cannot bear the truth he has revealed to them. He hadn't considered the social consequences of his actions. Unlike Brecht's Galileo, Fifty is no longer able to sit down, unconcerned, and enjoy his roast goose. For Canetti there is a difference between Fifty and Galileo, as he pointed out in *The Human Province.* "He lacks an entire dimension, which is precisely the one which has become important to us: What gives me the right to be the only one in possession of an explosive truth? Must I not try to render it harmless at any price? It is with me, the only bearer of this truth, that the process of dissolution, of neutralization, must begin." Brecht's attitude, based as it was on a materialistic interpretation of history, is not enough for Canetti. He wants to show that everything depends on the individual's readiness to change.

Already in 1933, Hermann Broch noted in an introductory speech to one of Canetti's public readings: "By confronting his characters, in the presence of his readers, with the fear of madness, he wants to achieve the kind of crushed remorse which can be compared only to Ekkehard's 'seclusion.' He wants to reduce man in his individuality, which is the seat not only of madness but also of sin—it's the old idea of obsession surfacing again and again—he wants to reduce the individual to point zero, to that final state of nothingness which must be reached in order to start anew again.''

Translated by Gitta Honegger

COMEDY OF VANITY

CHARACTERS*

Wenzel Wondrak, barker
Miss Bonnie May
Widow Holy ⟩ 3 best friends
Nurse Luise
Barass, packer
Anna Barass, his wife
François Fant, son of Emily Fant
Frankie Nada, an old public porter
Frances Nada, his sister
Hansi, Puppi, Gretl
Lizzi, Heidi, Lori ⟩ 6 little girls
Fritz Shakee, teacher
Emily Fant, mother
Henry Breeze
Leda Fresh ⟩ a couple
Eugene Kaldaun
Lya, his wife
Marie, maid of all work
Kaldaun Junior
Preacher Crumb
Theresa Shriek, owner of a general store
Millie Shriek, her daughter
Fred Hero, coiffeur
Joseph Killoff, director
S. Bleiss

*Note that the interchangeability of first and last names of the characters depends on the social context in which the scenes occur.

The songs used are popular tunes of the day, and selections from operettas. [Trans.]

PART I

WENZEL WONDRAK: (*The barker, on a completely empty stage.*) Now, we, ladies and gentlemen, yes, we, and we, and we, and we, ladies and gentlemen, and we, and we, we are going to do something. What are we going to do? We are going to do something terrific, absolutely terrific, something unheard of, something fantastic, gigantic, terrific! And we, ladies and gentlemen, we are absolutely terrific and we are up to something. What are we up to, ladies and gentlemen, yes, we and we and we, ladies and gentlemen? We think we're still here today, and here we are . . . today! But tomorrow we'll be gone, by tomorrow we'll have disappeared! See for yourself! Check it out! Cast your loving eye upon the eighth, the ninth, the tenth and the eleventh wonder of the world! I said eleven, but I won't say twelve. I'll say thirteen though, if you want me to! You aren't superstitious, are you, ladies and gentlemen? You aren't, are you? Are you superstitious? Come on in, ladies and gentlemen, I cordially request the pleasure of your company! You may even laugh if you want to, there's no law against laughing, laughing's still permitted. As a matter of fact, you are supposed to laugh, laugh like Bajazzo, which is the role I am planning to perform, with your kind permission, especially for you today!

Now we, and we, and we, ladies and gentlemen, yes, we, and we, ladies and gentlemen: you will have the chance, right here, to aim at your own faces. You'll be getting five balls, five round, hard balls, they're smooth, they're brand new! With your permission, you'll be getting these balls compliments of me, free of charge. Ladies and gentlemen, it'll be my pleasure to supply you with five balls. Who's going to pay? Not you. You don't have to pay, you can't pay, even if you wanted to. Because we, ladies and gentlemen, yes, we and we and we, we are going to pick up those balls . . . and what are we going to do with those balls? What are we aiming at? At your own faces! You've got your faces right in front of you, you'll be looking at your own lovely faces right there in those mirrors. You'll be aiming at your faces and you're going to smash your faces in all those mirrors. Just keep smashing as much as you want to. We have an endless supply of mirrors. There, in the back, people are arriving with their mirrors. Here, in front, they smash their faces in the mirrors. That is true virtue. That's what's called a noble heart. Because we, and we, and we, ladies and gentlemen, yes, we, we want to vanish, we want to completely disappear. Who'll have a try? Who'll have a shot at it? Are you vain, sir? Then come on in! And we, and we, yes, we, ladies and gentlemen, come try your luck, come on in, just come on in, it's not a sin, you'll feel holier than you've ever been. And we, and we, yes, we, ladies and gentlemen . . .

(*The revolving stage, with Wondrak standing on it, turns. His voice fades slowly. Miss Bonnie May, Widow Holy, Nurse Luise, three best friends, enter. Each is carrying a package wrapped in newspaper.*)

MAY: Did you count yours?
HOLY: Not me. I've got too many anyways.
LUISE: I'd say you are exaggerating.
HOLY: I'm telling you!
MAY: I counted mine.
HOLY: So, how many d'you have?
LUISE: That's what I'd like to know!
HOLY: And why should you care, Nurse Luise.
MAY: I can tell you.
HOLY: So, how many d'you have?
MAY: Guess.
HOLY: Let me see!
LUISE: That's nothing!
MAY: Look who's talking!
LUISE: I beg your pardon! I've got a lot more than her.

(*Miss May laughs shrilly, Widow Holy hollers.*)

LUISE: I've counted mine.
HOLY: Nurse Luise has counted hers. And she isn't even embarrassed.
LUISE: We'll soon see who's got the most!
HOLY: Miss Bonnie May, have you learned how to count yet!
MAY: You're three years older than me, right?

LUISE: Just show us your package.

HOLY: So, how many could you possibly have? Thirty, maybe!

LUISE: Never! Where would she get thirty? She has no family!

HOLY: If I count my brothers and sisters, that's nine right there. And I easily
have a dozen of each. So you can figure it out, if you want. Nine times
twelve, that's 84, no 108. Then add my late husband!

MAY: You don't have to have a family.

HOLY: Then where are you getting yours, if you don't have a family?

LUISE: I know. Bonnie May has her movie stars. She goes to the movies every
night and she sees every show at least three times.

MAY: Five times, if you really want to know.

HOLY: Well, now it's all over with the movies anyways.

LUISE: (*Reads from a huge poster, which up to now has been visible only in dim outlines.*)
Announcement. Point one. No. Point two. No. Point three. No. Point
four. Now: All movie theatres will be closed down. All reels, originals as
well as copies, will be destroyed. All productions of any kind of movie must
be stopped. Private showings are punishable with a minimum of eight years
in jail.

MAY: You really think you can hurt me, don't you?

LUISE: How could we? If there's no pride . . .

HOLY: There's nothing to hurt.

MAY: Alright, alright, I'll be hurt. Forever! I promise. But first let's count. I
insist that we count!

LUISE: Fine with me. I don't mind. I've been thrifty for the longest time. I always knew that it would come to this.

HOLY: I'd say: she who has least, will hurt the most.

MAY: It's really dirty here.

LUISE: Where? On that disgusting sidewalk?

HOLY: You and your cleanliness! Always talking about washing up. I don't
like washing myself all the time. And those packages'll be burned anyways.

LUISE: Fine with me. I don't mind.

MAY: Right on the sidewalk? (*Hesitates.*) Alright.

(*All three kneel down and put their packages in front of them. They untie the many, tightly
wrapped strings and proceed to count the contents. They count very quickly in order to reach
a high number as soon as possible. They count very slowly, because they are so fond of every
picture. They watch each other very closely. In fact everyone is counting the contents of all
three packages at the same time. Through their irregular mumbling one can hear an occasional loud crashing sound, screams and a roar as if from a large crowd.*)

LUISE: Wrong! You're only at 33.

HOLY: That's what I said. 33.

LUISE: No, you said 35, but you're only at 33.

HOLY: Thirty-four—that's Otto, my brother-in-law. (*Shows her a picture.*)

Dead. You never met him. He was a handsome devil. Cut his wrists. He always said, if he's gonna cut his wrists someday, it'll be my fault. He really loved me. Most handsome man we ever had in our family.—35, 36, 37.

MAY: Forty-six.—But nothing compared to Rudolfo Valentino. Will you look at him. What can I say—Gorgeous body and fire in his eyes—47, 48, 49.

LUISE: Fifty.—That's to be expected from a movie star.—50, 51, 52.

HOLY: Fifty.—Otherwise, every Tom, Dick and Harry'd be in the movies.—51, 52, 53.

LUISE: Fifty-seven.—Now this is Air Force Commander von Roennetal with his autograph dedicated to me. I nursed him. He always wanted to show his affection. What a gentleman. I nursed him back to health.—58, 59, 60.

MAY: Eighty.—Mariano Bello. Before his car accident. That's when he still had a gorgeous body and fire in his eyes. Afterwards, they had to stitch him together. There wasn't much left of him. 81, 82, 83.

HOLY: Seventy-eight.—My late husband, holding me in his lap. That's when he was really old: 25 and I was 5. He knew me even before I started school. He saw me once, at the photographer's and that's when he decided, right then and there, deep down in his heart: That's the one! So he waited for me for 15 years. And what did I get out of it? Nothing! He died two months after our wedding night. Handsome man! Very handsome man! But a bad heart. And so good-natured. Nothing could upset him. We got along so well.—Jesus 79, 80, 81.

LUISE: One hundred.—"Remember your grateful Theodor Buch, who is forever indebted to you." A noble man. I nursed him. He had never shown a woman his affection. That was his nature. He was 29. He confessed everything to me. I really would like to confess to you, Nurse Luise, he said.—101, 102, 103.

(*A loud male voice from the back jolts the women out of their activities.*)

BARASS: Here take this one. You gonna move? No? I'm gonna punch ya again. There! How's that, huh? Yes, sirreeh, I've got the devil in my fists, you've got no chance. Wham! Bam! You felt that one, didn't ya, that one hurt. Wanna play games with me? You gotta be kidding! There . . . take that . . . and that . . . and another one!

(*In the meantime, Barass, the packer, has reached the stage. With his fat fists he punches a huge bale, which is neatly tied with ropes. Anna, his wife, a scrawny, whining figure, is running behind him. She tries in vain to grasp at the ropes to hold back the bale.*)

ANNA: You can't do that. It ain't right.

BARASS: What ain't right? I'm always right. I'll smash the whole city, if I goddam please. That's right, the whole goddam city! (*He emphasizes each sentence with a punch.*)

ANNA: Something awful's gonna happen!

BARASS: What? What's gonna happen? Nothing's gonna happen. That's gotta burn and it's gonna burn.

ANNA: But it don't belong to you.

BARASS: So who's gonna throw it in the fire? Me!

ANNA: That's theft. You're stealing someone else's property!

BARASS: Property? Property! You call this property? This ain't no property. This is a crime!

ANNA: I can hear them come! I'm so scared!

BARASS: You just watch when they come. I'll be the hero. You just watch!

(*One can hear many people approaching. Through the noise it sounds as if they are murmuring "Barass, Barass."*)

ANNA: Now you've really done it. I'm so scared!

BARASS: Take it easy, honeybun! You know what I'm gonna say to them? I won't say a word. But I'm gonna give a speech! Gentlemen, I'll say, I won't take this no more! I'm here working like a slave, doing your job. You oughta be doing this, but who's doing it? Me! I've been in the apartments, I took the photographs. Ain't they illegal? So what's the difference if they burn now or later? They're illegal, ain't they. The forbidden fruit. It ain't right. And the fruit, the fruit of my labor, gentlemen, is wrapped in this package. It's much too small, 'cause I didn't have the time for all the other buildings. Now you tell me yourself, am I right or ain't I!

(*The noise has passed. The three women had been too amazed to count. Suddenly, Widow Holy reaches into the pictures which are piled up on the sidewalk and grabs as many as she can to carry them to Barass with her arms stretched toward him. On her way over, she says loudly, "Handsome fella." She puts the pictures on top of Barass's bale.*)

HOLY: There, you take those too. You are so right! I'm with you all the way. We wanted to take them there ourselves, me and my two girl friends over there. But you take them!

(*Nurse Luise and Miss Bonnie May shrug somewhat hesitatingly.*)

BARASS: I like you.

HOLY: Handsome devil!

BARASS: I like you! Quite a woman, you! (*Grabs her at the shoulders and the back.*) Not just skin 'n' bones like her (*points scornfully back to his wife*).

ANNA: Now you really did it! Now you can drag her along, too!

LUISE: (*Tears in her eyes.*) Look—he's showing his affection.

MAY: (*Haltingly.*) You call that a body? And where's the fire in the eyes?

LUISE: Still, he's showing his affection.

(*Both carry the rest of the pictures over to him.*)

LUISE: Here you go. We don't mind. Here are 174, they're mine and here are 166 from Bonnie May. Widow Holy has close to 150.

HOLY: So what if I got the least.

BARASS: It's all gonna go in the fire. It'll all be burning soon. Come on, gimme a hand, everybody. Believe me, I could do without you. I've got the devil in my arms. Believe me, I could handle three times as much. But I ain't greedy. C'mon, help me, everybody. (*To Widow Holy.*) Go on, you're first! (*He slaps her back.*)

LUISE: (*Who gives a helping hand.*) Me too, please.

ANNA: So now everybody's helping. So why the hell did you work your butt off before?

MAY: (*Who stays behind with Anna Barass, overwhelmed.*) Gorgeous body and fire in his eyes.

ANNA: Now you did it.

(*The barker can be heard from afar: "Now we, and we and we, yes, we, ladies and gentlemen!" François Fant, in all his youthful elegance, enters lightfootedly. Gasping right behind him under a heavy load of mirrors is Frankie Nada, an old porter.*)

NADA: Heavy, young man, heavy.

FANT: Just keep going. You'll make it.

NADA: If I had known that you own that many mirrors! And heavy ones.

FANT: My dear friend, it's up to you.

NADA: I'm only saying . . .

FANT: (*Stops.*) By the way, if you don't want to go on, I can always find someone else!

NADA: (*Petrified.*) Beg your kindness, young man, I didn't mean it. At my age. No need to get angry.

FANT: Well then.

NADA: Ogodogodogod!

FANT: What is it now?

NADA: Nothing.

FANT: Where on earth are you? Can't you hurry up?

NADA: I think I won't make it.

FANT: If you keep carrying on like this, I might just carry some myself.

NADA: For the love of God, don't do that to me. I couldn't bear the shame. At my age! If my sister would find out about this! I've been a public porter for 56 years.

FANT: So, let's go!

NADA: It's only my age.

FANT: We all do what we can.

NADA: You're right, young man. When, uh, I still had my sister . . .

FANT: Only a couple of blocks.

NADA: I'm coming, I'm coming. My sister's name's Frances and I am Frank.

FANT: Let's go now. We'll be late.

NADA: Ready—go.

FANT: That's the way. We all do what we can. Everybody's sacrificing something. I'm sacrificing all my mirrors. That's 14, altogether. You help me carry the mirrors because you have nothing else to sacrifice. Not everybody can make such a big sacrifice. How much would you think these mirrors are worth?

NADA: I'd say they're worth a fortune! My sister Frances, God bless her . . .

FANT: What's your guess?

NADA: Oh—an unbelievable fortune! Frances, my . . .

FANT: You bet. "Fortune" is an understatement. And I'm going to smash them all, singlehandedly, with a ball, that is. Fantastic!

NADA: (*Gasping for air.*)

FANT: Watch it! Here comes a stone. Make sure they don't break. Watch it, you hear! Be more careful with my mirrors, will you!

(*Nada keeps gasping and gasping.*)

FANT: (*Screaming.*) It'll only take three more minutes. Come, come! Three minutes. Then you can loaf as much as you want.

(*Nada collapses, the mirrors crash.*)

FANT: (*Angrily.*) That's all I needed! One should have no pity. I should've gotten someone else, it wouldn't have cost me anything either. (*With his foot, he kicks the old man out of the way.*) Did he wreck them all? One, two, three, four, five, six, seven, eight. Eight are alright. Could've been worse. But who's going to carry them over for me?

(*Frances Nada, an old maidservant comes dragging in.*)

FANT: Where are you headed, grandma?

FRANCES: I want to see the celebration. I can't bring anything. But at least I can watch.

FANT: Wait, maybe I can help you. You take the mirrors, eight altogether, so you can bring something too.

FRANCES: I don't believe it! I just don't believe it! I really get those eight mirrors. I don't believe it. I just don't believe it!

FANT: (*Loading her with the mirrors.*) What a pity they had to break.

FRANCES: I'll be careful, don't worry, young man, sir, I'll be very careful. Don't you worry, sir. I even had a brother who was a public porter.

FANT: Are they well stacked?

FRANCES: Yes, sir! Thank you kindly, sir. My brother, you know, the one who was a porter, I lost him thirty years ago. Thank you kindly, sir. I thought I might meet him at the celebration, because a porter should do a lot of business there.

FANT: That's very interesting. But now let's go! What a pity about those mirrors!

FRANCES: Thank you kindly, sir. I can't believe it. Thank you so much, sir! Bless you, sir, bless you, bless you, young man, sir!

FANT: What a pity. I could've brought 14 mirrors.

FRANCES: Bless you kindly, sir. Such a sweet, kind, fine young man!

(As she exits, the Barker can be heard: "Now we, and we, and we, ladies and gentlemen, yes we . . ." Nada gets up with great difficulty and checks his old bones.)

NADA: At my age! It's so embarrassing! If my Frances could see me now!

(Six little girls come skipping in.)

HANSI: I can come.

PUPPI: I can come too.

GRETL: She can't come!

PUPPI: Oh yes, I can!

GRETL: No, she can't!

HANSI: I can come.

LIZZI: Look, everybody. Look what I have!

HANSI, PUPPI, GRETL: Let's see!

LIZZI: No, I'm not showing you.

HEIDI: If you show me, you can have a lick. *(Holds up a lollipop.)*

LIZZI: First I wanna lick.

HEIDI: All right. *(Solemn licking.)*

LIZZI: Now I'll show you. But only you. They can't look.

GRETL: Greedy!

LORI: *(Who up to now has been watching quietly, a little further away from the others.)* She got nothing to show you.

LIZZI: *(Turning around quickly.)* Well, I won't show you, that's for sure!

HANSI, PUPPI, GRETL: She got nothing to show, she's only pretending.

LIZZI: Come here, everybody, I'll show you. But not that big bully, she can't look.

(Hansi, Puppi, Gretl run over to her. Lori moves scornfully even further away. Now Hansi, Puppi, Gretl run excitedly to Lori, they talk loudly, all at once.)

GRETL: She has a picture of her father.

HANSI: He lets her burn it.

PUPPI: And she has a picture of her mother.

HEIDI: And of her big brother.

GRETL: They gave them to her.

PUPPI: I didn't get any.

GRETL: You can't come, anyways.

PUPPI: (*Starts to cry.*) I can too!

LIZZI: Leave her alone. I'll take her. She can come with me.

(*Embarrassed pause from the others. Puppi is laughing again.*)

LIZZI: (*To Lori.*) So, what do you say now? Now you don't know what to say! Can't you say something? You've got nothing to say! That's my daddy. That's my mommy. And that's my big brother.

LORI: I bet you stole them.

LIZZI: (*Hits her in the face.*) You're so mean! It's alright to be mean, my daddy says. But not that mean!

LORI: (*Laughs scornfully.*) How many d'you have? Three? (*She pulls a package out of her blouse.*) I've got twenty-three! And I didn't steal them either. My mother's sick, so I'm going for her to the celebration.

(*The girls are joining Lori.*)

LIZZI: (*To Puppi.*) You're going with her too?

PUPPI: She's got twenty-three.

LORI: Come with me, I'll take you. You can come with me.

LIZZI: I'll give you the picture of my brother.

(*Puppi hesitates.*)

LORI: And you'll throw it in the fire, all right?

PUPPI: I can throw your brother in the fire?

LORI: No, not my brother. I'll give you my mother. You can throw her in.

HANSI: I'll take it.

GRETL: Me too.

HEIDI: Me too.

PUPPI: It's mine now!

LORI: C'mon. Stay here, I'll give you two pictures. (*She removes the package from inside her blouse and takes out two pictures, which she gives to Puppi.*)

PUPPI: (*Waves the two pictures in front of the others.*) Now I've got two!

HANSI: I want some too!

GRETL: Me too!

HEIDI: Me too!

LIZZI: You can have my mommy, if I can have another lick!

HEIDI: Alright.

LORI: C'mon. Stay here. You can have two pictures too. (*Again she produces the package from inside her blouse and also gives Heidi two pictures.*)
HEIDI: (*Pushes Puppi.*) Now I've got two!

(*Hansi and Gretl are ready to cry.*)

LIZZI: (*Goes to them.*) I'll give you my mommy. She is for both of you.

(*Hansi and Gretl curl their noses; nonetheless, they do hold out their hands.*)

LORI: (*Steps in.*) I'll give you both two pictures too. (*Same procedure as before.*)

(*Hansi and Gretl turn their backs to Lizzi.*)

LORI: Now you all have to come with me. If you have my pictures, you have to come with me.
HANSI: Who wants to go with her?
PUPPI: Not me.
GRETL: Her and her mother!
HEIDI: She can keep her mother.
LIZZI: My mommy is beautiful.
GRETL: She's cross-eyed.
LIZZI: (*Hits her in the face.*) You're so mean!
GRETL: (*Hits her back.*) She's cross-eyed and she's ugly and she's got a big nose and she's got a limp and she's hunchbacked and smells bad on top of that! My mother says you can't stay in the same room with her, she smells so bad. And she's cross-eyed and has an ugly nose!
HANSI: I saw it too.
HEIDI: In the picture.
PUPPI: Me too.

(*Lizzi cries and keeps hitting Gretl who cries and keeps insulting her mother. Lori laughs and the others watch. Fritz Shakee, a teacher, but not the teacher of these children, appears on the scene.*)

SHAKEE: Ch-ch-children a-a-aren't s-s-supposed t-t-o be h-h-ere. Ch-ch-children a-a-re s-s-supposed t-t-to b-be at h-h-home.

(*All six girls freeze.*)

SHAKEE: H-h-hurry on h-h-home, I s-s-say. D-d-do I h-h-ave t-to sh-show y-y-you? Ch-ch-ch-ildren a-a-aren't s-s-suposed t-t-to b-be h-here.
LORI: (*Steps forward.*) My mother is sick and she sent me with 23 pictures. They all go into the big fire.

(*The others hold up their pictures tentatively.*)

SHAKEE: How m-m-many?

LORI: Twenty-three. (*She takes all the pictures, which she had given to Hansi, Puppi, Gretl, and Heidi, who don't dare to resist.*) My mother said.

SHAKEE: B-b-because of t-t-twenty th-th-three l-l-lousy ph-ph-photos sh-she s-s-sends y-you out in th-th-the st-streets? G-g-give them t-t-to m-m-me, I'll th-th-throw th-them in. (*He snatches the package from Lori.*) Y-y-you've-ve s-s-something too! (*To Lizzi.*) G-give th-th-them t-t-to me. (*He takes Lizzi's three little pictures. She desperately holds on to them. Three tiny scraps remain in her hand.*)

(*As if on cue, the six girls start to cry, heartbreakingly and endlessly.*)

SHAKEE: Now g-g-get lost. Wh-wh-what are y-you w-w-waiting f-for? G-g-get l-l-lost, I said!

(*The girls hold on to each other, as he chases them away, punching them with his hard, bony fists. Their screams merge with the noises from the fair in the background, and fade into the screams of a woman. Emily Fant, a very fat woman, made up brightly and decked out with jewelry, runs across the stage, gesticulating wildly.*)

MME. FANT: My child! Where's my child? My child ran away. Where can I find my child? Has anyone seen my child? My child! Here I am, working, slaving day and night, night and day, day and night, one would think I'd be rolling in money. And for what? That's no way to work. Did I deserve this? My child! Where's my child? My child ran away. Where can I find my child? Did anyone see my child?

SHAKEE: (*Who has been standing to the side, walks now stiffly to the woman and stammers:*) T-t-today is a-a-a b-big d-day! S-stop s-screaming!

MME. FANT: (*Notices him only now and throws herself on him, screaming.*) You've seen my child! Where's my child? You know it! I know, you know it!

SHAKEE: S-s-stop s-screaming! I d-didn't!

MME. FANT: How can I stop screaming? I want the whole world to know! My only child! And all my work, for whom? Tell me where my child is. You know it. I know you know it.

SHAKEE: I d-d-don't h-have th-the p-pictures.

MME. FANT: My pictures? He doesn't have my pictures. Who's talking about my pictures? He's got my mirrors. Fourteen mirrors! He took them out of my house! Every one of my fourteen mirrors! How can my girls do their job without my mirrors? That's no way to work. I can't work that way. My girls are desperate.

SHAKEE: (*Has grown in size during her last words. He pulls a piece of paper out of his pocket and reads with a high, loud voice without stammering once.*) Public Notice:

The Government has decided: Point One: The possession and use of mirrors is prohibited. All extant mirrors must be destroyed. All manufacture of mirrors must be stopped. If after a period of thirty days a person is found still to possess or use a mirror, he or she will be punished with ten to twelve years imprisonment. The manufacture of mirrors carries the death penalty.

MME. FANT: The death penalty. I see. I would have given six of my mirrors, voluntarily, even without asking for any compensation. But all of my mirrors? Fourteen altogether! That's impossible. I can't work that way. Who can? Just ask my girls!

SHAKEE: Oh-oh b-be q-quiet! Point Two: The taking of pictures of human and related beings is strictly prohibited. All extant photographs of human or related beings will be destroyed. Until further notice, all photographic equipment must be turned in at the nearest government agency. The production of photographic equipment must be terminated as of today. After a period of thirty days, anyone still possessing any photographs of human or related beings will be punished with three to five years imprisonment. The taking of pictures of human and related beings carries the death penalty.

MME. FANT: The death penalty. I see. I can't hand in my pictures. My girls need their pictures for their customers. You can't get a decent customer without first showing him these pictures. That's no way to work. I can't work without my pictures. As if I were rolling in money!

SHAKEE: B-b-be qu-quiet. Point Three: The creation of portraits or self-portraits in oil, water color, charcoal, pencil or any other medium is strictly prohibited. Until further notice, all extant portraits or self-portraits must be turned in at the nearest government agency. Most of them are to be destroyed. A committee of experts will select a few for the permanent collection of the Museum of Vanity which is now in its planning stages. After a period of thirty days, the possession of portraits or self-portraits is punishable with eight to ten years imprisonment. The creation of portraits or self-portraits carries the death penalty.

MME. FANT: The death penalty! The death penalty! Nothing but death penalties! Now I've really had it. You think I can stand here all day?! Did you see my son François, yes or no? You couldn't have possibly missed him with my fourteen mirrors, huge ones! You must've seen him!

SHAKEE: B-b-be q-quiet. Point Four . . .

MME. FANT: Leave me alone, will you! I can't stand here all day! Listening to your nonsense! What does that buy me? What am I supposed to do? Put my girls out in the street, yes!? You certainly have no heart! I've got to get my mirrors back. I am a working woman. How am I supposed to do my work? No heart, that's you!

SHAKEE: (*Crowing.*) Point Four: (*She won't let him continue.*) Y-y-you w-w-watch i-it! I-I a-am g-going t-to r-report y-you!

MME. FANT: (*As she is running off.*) No heart! As if I were rolling in money! My child! Where's my child! My child ran away! Has anyone seen my child?

My child!

(As soon as he starts stammering, Shakee shrinks again. He positions himself on the side, as before. Henry Breeze and Leda Fresh are strolling in, involved in a conversation.)

BREEZE: I beg your pardon, dear lady, but that's exactly what this is NOT about. This is not a question of petty rules and regulations which are supposed to get us from one day to the next. We can't always be content with just getting by, although we've gotten so used to just getting by, it's become our second nature. But that'll have to change.

LEDA: I read about that in the paper yesterday. You're probably right, I s'ppose.

BREEZE: But not because you've read about it, dear lady. I have no idea where you've read it. I don't quote, I don't need to borrow my thoughts from others, I've got my own, as you should know. No, no, we are talking about a totally different way of life on a much higher level of consciousness. Just take a close look at life as it used to be. What was the first thing people did when they got out of bed? They washed themselves. Where? In front of a mirror. They combed their hair. Where? In front of a mirror. They shaved. Where? In front of a mirror!

LEDA: They put on makeup. Where? In front of a mirror. They powdered their noses. Where? In front of a mirror.

BREEZE: I am delighted to point out that your kidding actually supports my argument. Without even noticing it, you immediately switched to examples from a woman's life, which is all I need to prove my point. We have become effeminate. That is our tragedy. The mirror, a woman's tool of trade, has taken over the lives of all of us, including men. We no longer forge ahead as we used to; instead, we spend the best part of our days looking at ourselves with such intensity as if we had to paint a self-portrait: We do it with a passion as if we wanted to make love to our own image. Indeed, this has gone so far that sooner or later we actually enter into marriage with ourselves. Oh yes, every one of us is wedded to his mirror image. When we eat, we nourish our image; when we dress, we dress our image and if we are sick and down and miserable we make sure our image is in good health, or life would really lose all its meaning for us.

LEDA: I love to hear you talk like this. It adds a certain aura of virility, I s'ppose.

BREEZE: Doesn't it! Really! But what is at stake is far more important than myself. Still, your observation may give you a clue. Talking about our great common cause, about our war against mirrors, makes me appear . . . more virile, as you say.

LEDA: Yes, like a warrior, I s'ppose. Victorious.

BREEZE: You really think so? Victorious?

LEDA: A smile on his strong lips even as he dies.

BREEZE: Strong lips? Alright. If you insist. Yes. But what were we talking about?

LEDA: About female vanity, which has become a male obsession too, I s'ppose.

BREEZE: Right! Now I ask you, is it any different with photographs? Shamelessly we pose in front of some dark hole, and we contort our faces, faces, mind you, which might not even be all that bad, but we contort them to sugar-coated masks, and in most cases these masks have been forced on us by none other than the photographers themselves. Photographs are a compromise between the vanities of the photographer and his model. Perhaps we love them so much because we can look at ourselves as often as we like. And those stupid scrapbooks which we keep opening, three hundred times maybe, to exhibit ourselves to others, again and again, from birth to death—aren't they the most embarrassing invention of the vanity-devil?

LEDA: I don't know. I rather like baby pictures, I s'ppose. Don't you have any pictures from your childhood?

BREEZE: Of course I do. Why?

LEDA: I would've liked to see them. I bet you were a little dynamo even as a child.

BREEZE: That's what my family keeps saying. I was unusually precocious, they say, and I could read already at the age of four. You should hear the stories they tell about me. Amazing! When I was five, they say, I was sitting on my father's back while he was reading the newspaper to me and I actually corrected him!

LEDA: How cute. That's the cutest story I ever heard. What a charming little dynamo! Correcting his father's mistakes! How absolutely charming! (*She manages to force herself into his arms.*)

BREEZE: (*While he lets her have her way.*) Would you call this charming too?

(*In the meantime, Fritz Shakee has tried desperately to gasp for air, he has swallowed several times, opened and moved his mouth; he pulled out a piece of paper and practiced reading it in a low voice. Just as the two embrace, he feels secure enough to address them. He walks over to them stiffly and croaks:*)

SHAKEE: Y-y-you a-a-are a-a-b-bsolutely r-r-right! (*Henry Breeze and Leda Fresh move apart quickly.*) H-h-have y-y-you s-seen th-this? (*He holds up the piece of paper and crows again, without a stammer.*) "The hazardous rise of vanity in all walks of life, both private and public, can no longer be tolerated. Glitter and glamor, follies and fads control our lives. Everyone has made it his highest goal to appear and act like a peacock."

BREEZE: Thanks. I've seen it.

SHAKEE: Th-the l-lady d-doesn't know it-t. "Our shop windows are filled with false gods. All the misery in the world is choking in luxury. No one has the strength and stamina to sustain simplicity."

BREEZE: Thank you very much. The lady knows it too. Really.

LEDA: I s'ppose, I do.

SHAKEE: D-d-do y-you kn-kn-know this? "A bunch of howling baboons with glaring red asses, feathers on their heads and rings through their noses are roaming the streets and polluting the air."

BREEZE: Yes, I know. And I know a lot more.

LEDA: My fiancée knows everything, I s'ppose. (*Leda and Henry walk faster.*)

SHAKEE: (*Keeping in step with them.*) B-b-but y-y-you d-d-don't kn-know this, I-I b-bet. "The nation is doomed to fall."

BREEZE: I know it. I know it all.

LEDA: My fiancée knows everything.

SHAKEE: "Who could claim under oath that he doesn't carry a mirror in his pocket?"

(*The Kaldaun family consists of four members: Eugene Kaldaun is lost in thoughts. His wife Lya is preoccupied with her pocketbook; Marie, their maid-of-all-work, just about past her prime, is walking behind them, pushing the baby carriage which contains Kaldaun Junior.*)

LYA: Eugene, what shall I sacrifice today?

EUGENE: These pants haven't been ironed again!

LYA: Eugene, what shall I sacrifice today?

EUGENE: I am talking about my pants. These pants haven't been ironed. Simple as that.

LYA: Do you think, I should sacrifice my compact mirror today?

EUGENE: I don't have to put up with this. Those pants have not been ironed.

LYA: Marie, you aren't listening. Those pants have not been ironed. My husband, Mr. Kaldaun, doesn't have to put up with this.

EUGENE: So why don't you contribute your mirror, if that's what you want. Simple as that.

LYA: Should I, really? I'm not sure.

EUGENE: I'm not sure if I can show up like this.

LYA: Marie, my husband, Mr. Kaldaun, is too embarrassed to show up like this. Do you hear? My husband! Mr. Kaldaun!

EUGENE: I'd bring the mirror, if I were you. It'll look good. Embarrassing, really.

LYA: What do you think? Mr. Kaldaun, my husband, is going to the fair just for the fun of it? Marie, what's going on in that head of yours?

EUGENE: You must pull it out very quickly: a sudden decision. Simple as that. And I'm supposed to be embarrassed?! I won't have it.

LYA: You see, Marie. For the hundreth time! Mr. Kaldaun, my husband, has had it! He won't have it! But then, what am I going to do with it, Eugene?

EUGENE: You just throw it in the fire. That'll look good. Simple as that. You have to throw it when everybody's watching. Right into the fire. No one's going to wreck my nerves anymore. I've had it. Look at those creases, will you! Right into the fire.

KALDAUN JR.: (*Suddenly screaming.*) Fy-ah! Fy-ahh!

(*As the scene moves closer to the fire, its reddish glow gradually intensifies. The voices surrounding it seem to be getting closer, they sound more excited.*)

LYA: I just take it and throw it right into the fire. Marie. When was the last time you ironed Mr. Kaldaun's pants?

JUNIOR: Fy-aahh! Fy-aaahhh!

MARIE: (*Czech accent.*) Is not so bad. Today in the morning, before Sir put them on. Pants were ironed today in the morning and pants are just right. I quit. Just so you know! Pants!

(*She leaves the carriage in the middle of the street. Her hands barely let go of it, when Junior starts screaming at the top of his lungs.*)

JUNIOR: Fy-ah-yah-yah-yah! Fy-ah-yah-yah-yah!

LYA: Am I supposed to calm down the baby, Marie? I don't have time now. I have to throw the mirror right into the fire. Eugene, what shall I tell her? Why don't you take care of it! Will you, please.

EUGENE: Marie, I am telling you for the hundredth time: You stay! Simple as that.

JUNIOR: Fy-ah-yah-yah-yah!

(*Marie gets back to the carriage and pushes it again.*)

LYA: Eugene, shall I take out the mirror now?

EUGENE: Wait, till we stand right in front of it, that'll look better.

JUNIOR: (*Triumphantly.*) Fy-aahh! Fy-aaahhh!

(*The Kaldauns have now reached the square with the fire burning to the right. It is getting bigger by the minute. The barker's stall is located upstage left. One wouldn't pay any attention to it, were it not for the continuous sound of crashing mirrors, which one doesn't get used to as quickly as the barker's voice. Many people are milling between the fire and the mirror-crashing, among them all the characters we have met before with the exception of the six little girls. A stocky preacher with a fat face stands on top of a soapbox next to the fire. He is drawing the largest crowd.*)

PREACHER CRUMB: But we don't want to prattle, we want to battle! Brothers and sisters, let us battle the heinous vice of vanity! Satan's holding us in his ugly green claws. He holds on to us tightly and he's gnawing on us like on an old crust o' bread. He's gaggin' 'n' spittin', but he can't get us down his throat. Go ahead, look at him, brothers and sisters, what do you see? We are too rotten even for the devil. He's tryin', he's chewin', he's retchin' till his ugly red face's turning green just like his ugly claws. He's hissin', he's cussin', but not even the devil can help, 'cause he is the devil and he's got to swallow us. But we are poison to him, we're the worst poison for the devil. Now I can hear you ask: How come? How come not even the devil can swallow us? How come we are such poison even to the devil? Isn't he the devil? Isn't he much worse than we? Let me tell you, my poor brothers and sisters! The devil's bad, the devil's rotten, but the devil doesn't carry a little mirror in his pocket and he doesn't have any photographs and he doesn't have any pictures. Believe me, I've spent a lot of time with him. I've reached into his red-hot pockets, I've searched his bag of dirty tricks, I've been down his gory caverns, I've been in his darkest torture chambers, I've been to hell, oh yes, I've searched all over—and believe me, hell's a big place, there's much room down there, and it's gettin' bigger by the hour. But I haven't found a mirror anywhere, not even the tiniest mirror, nowhere! Nowhere! In hell there are no mirrors! Only we have mirrors and pictures and photographs, and he who poses in front of the camera is much worse than the devil. Not even hell has any room for him. So where is he going to roast? Where is his soul going to end up? I can't tell you that. But we don't want to prattle, we want to battle. Brothers and sisters, let us battle the . . .

(*A shrill noise emerges from the general noise: "Now this one and this one and this one and this one!" The stage turns slightly, the glow of the fire is still very intense, only the crowd isn't quite as large.*)

THERESA SHRIEK: (*Owner of a general store, tears up her photographs and throws the pieces in the direction of the fire.*) Now this one and this one and this one!
MILLI: (*Her daughter.*) What are you doing Mama?
THERESA: Now this one and this one and this one!
FRED HERO: (*Coiffeur, who stands next to her.*) One at a time!
MILLI: Mama, did you throw my picture too?
THERESA: I'll get to it. I'll get to it. Now this one and this one and this one!
MILLI: But the pictures of me—you don't have to throw them all in today. Mommie, please . . .
THERESA: Especially your pictures! 'Cause vanity sits in your flesh like the worm in the apple."
MILLI: But I just had them done, for Freddy, those beautiful pictures!
THERESA: He knows your face, he doesn't need your pictures.
MILLI: He told me, he loves me because of the pictures. Mama, what are you doin'? Stop it Mama!
THERESA: We can do without Freddy.
MILLI: Now she's tearin' him up too! Now she's tearin' up my Freddy! Don't Mama, please!
HERO: My name is Fred, if you don't mind.

MILLI: Mama! Don't!

HERO: If you don't mind, my name is Fred.

MILLI: Mama, what are you doin'? Mama, please, what are you doin'? Now she's torn up Freddy! She's torn up my Freddy!

HERO: If you don't mind, there's always another Fred. For example, my name's Fred too, if you don't mind.

MILLI: My Freddy won't come back. (*Sobbing bitterly.*) If he can't find his picture, he'll never come back.

HERO: Finished, as they say. Mind you, am I not a handsome Fred?

MILLI: Why d'you keep introducing yourself? What d'you want from me? I don't even know you.

HERO: Permit me to offer you, very discretely, a picture of Fred.

MILLI: Go on! Show me! Where'd you get it?

HERO: I must ask for your discretion. We are being watched.

MILLI: We are being watched. That's what Freddy always said.

HERO: Shouldn't we go over to the side?

MILLI: First show me the picture.

HERO: With pleasure.

MILLI: That ain't Freddy.

HERO: You are holding the picture of a gentleman whose name is Fred.

MILLI: But that's you.

HERO: As I said, my name is Fred.

MILLI: So, what's that gotta do with me?

HERO: With your permission, I want you to keep this picture.

MILLI: What did you say? I can keep the picture?

HERO: If you don't mind.

MILLI: It's all mine? You're kidding!

HERO: All yours. Just like my heart. Shouldn't we step to the side?

MILLI: If I can keep the picture, why not!

HERO: As I said.

MILLI: It's really a beautiful picture, Freddy!

THERESA: Now this one and this one and this one and this one!

PREACHER CRUMB: There's plenty of animals in this world, mammals and birds and snakes, no human alive could name them all. But I know one animal that's filthier than all the others. You've got it on your mind day and night and you don't mind at all. Now you tell me the name of that animal, you tell me yourself, I'm asking you: Vanity, what is your real name?

(*In a more quiet spot, but not far from the fire, Joseph Killoff, Director, smiles benevolently in all directions. He is alone.*)

KILLOFF: Will you look at that! What a fire! Nice. I like it. Fire. That red glow. And the people—they're going crazy. Just give them a spectacle and they'll come running, they love it. Well, why not, they're only human.

Those pictures make a great fire. Look at those flames. No great loss, all those pictures in that fire. But you keep yours nice and safe. (*He pulls out a small pocket-size mirror and looks at himself carefully, for a long time.*) It all makes sense for the masses. They'll waste their last hard-earned nickel. They never know when to stop. (*Slowly, he puts the mirror back in his pocket.*) Boy, is this making me sweat. Three weeks ago . . . you remember. I am passing a photographer's studio. He's got a car standing in front of his shop. Now I have this habit—I think: What's this car doing in front of his shop? So I sit down on the bench and I wait. Soon enough, a young couple arrives, they hold hands, they embrace, he hasn't got a penny, she hasn't got a penny, they have their picture taken in front of the car. The newlyweds' capital investment: A car.

How d'you like that. I mean, really. So now, when they meet someone who might ask them: what do you do for a living? they can answer: we own a car. And they can prove it with the photographs which they carry in their wallets. How d'you like that. But that's all over now my dear newly-wed car owners. You may own a car or you may not own a car, it makes no difference anymore. You can stick your nice pictures right into the fire, because up-you-know-where would be against the law . . . Now where did I put mine? (*He takes a stack of pictures from his wallet and looks at them carefully, tenderly.*) Now I'd like to know: does my nose look like that? (*Points to a picture.*) Or like that? (*Points to another one.*) We'll find out right away. (*Takes out his mirror again and holds it between the two noses in question.*) Just one moment please. Gee. It does look like that. I wouldn't have thought so. I mean, really. How d'you like that. Maybe it's the fire, of course, it's the glow of the fire. Just look at that fire! That's a hungry fire, better watch it. (*He turns away from the fire, less friendly now, and puts away his pictures with great affection.*) Just a bit too hot for me. Well, my friend—you see, the masses'll spend their last hard-earned nickel. They don't know when to stop. (*He takes another look at himself in the mirror.*) Now I'm all red from that fire. What a fire.

BLEISS: (*Behind him.*) Have you got any left?

KILLOFF: (*Taken by surprise, turns around angrily.*) What?

BLEISS: Have you any left? If you do, give them to me.

KILLOFF: What'm I supposed to have?

BLEISS: Give them to me. I pay top prices.

KILLOFF: I'd really like to know what you want from me, mister!

BLEISS: Nothing. Nothing. I'm just asking if you have any left. I buy. Everything. Whatever you have, give it to me.

KILLOFF: There's nothing to buy here and nothing to sell, mister!

BLEISS: Maybe some of the wife, a few of the children, of the family. I pay more by the dozen.

KILLOFF: (*Screams.*) What makes you think I'm married, mister! Married!? A man like me? Do you think I'm stupid?!

BLEISS: Alright, not married, but there's a lady friend, maybe two, one blond, one black. What's going to happen to them?

KILLOFF: I have no lady friend. How d'you like that! I rather spend my money on myself.

BLEISS: But you, you are such a handsome man, you've got class, you must have hundreds, of yourself, I mean. I pay more by the hundred.

KILLOFF: You've never heard of ideals, have you? This is no place to peddle, this is the place to burn! This country's had enough of you leeches! I know what you used to be. A photographer! Now I remember you! You're the one with the car. You're a photographer! (*Bleiss disappears quickly.*) How d'you like that! A photographer and dares to show his face in public!

PREACHER CRUMB: Vanity is a sow! A big, fat, stinking sow. Look at her, decked out with glitter 'n' gew-gaw! Look at her sparkle and shine and strut like a peacock! It won't do her any good! We know who it is. 'Cause we recognize her snout! She's put bright red lipstick on her snout and now she puckers it and sticks it in our faces. Now where do you think she likes it best? In the dirt, that's where! In the dirt. Tear the glitter off her body, rip off her glittering slough and see what's left, brothers and sisters. Underneath the slough you find an ugly, stinking sow! Vanity is a sow . . .

(*Frances Nada, very tiny and bent over, sneaks quickly across the square. She disappears and right away comes back again, exactly the same way as before, as if looking for something she has lost.*)

FRITZ SHAKEE: (*Crowing.*) H-h-hold i-i-t! W-w-what a-a-are y-y-you d-doing?

(*Frances startles and trembles in tiny, subservient twitches.*)

SHAKEE: Wh-wh-what are you doing?

(*Frances trembles.*)

SHAKEE: I-I'm a-asking you wh-what y-you a-a-are doing!

FRANCES: Beg you beg you beg you beg you beg your pardon, young man, sir.

SHAKEE: Y-y-you were being w-w-watched. Y-y-you've been looking f-f-for something.

FRANCES: Beg you beg you beg your pardon, young man, sir.

SHAKEE: D'you w-want t-to deny it?

FRANCES: I beg your pardon, sir.

SHAKEE: Y-you've b-been l-looking for half an h-hour. Wh-what have you been looking for?

FRANCES: Beg your pardon, sir, my brother, sir.

SHAKEE: Your b-brother. Th-that's a good one. G-g-give it to me.

FRANCES: But I can't find him. Beg your pardon, young man, sir, I just can't find him.

SHAKEE: Very well. You are asking f-f-for it! G-g-give it to me!

FRANCES: What do you want from my brother, sir? Do you need a porter?

SHAKEE: Your b-brother b-belongs in the f-f-fire. G-g-give it to me!

FRANCES: (*Howling at the top of her lungs, she has stopped trembling.*) You can't have my brother! Not my brother! No! Never!

SHAKEE: You are under arrest. C-come with me!

FRANCES: Not my brother! Never. Not my brother . . . (*Fading away.*)

HENRY BREEZE: She lacks the sense for the seriousness of this hour. I . . .

LEDA FRESH: She's too old for that, I s'ppose. My . . .

FRANKIE NADA: The old lady's sure screaming her head off. What's the matter with her, young man, sir?

BREEZE: (*Benevolently to the old man.*) She's been arrested. (*To Leda Fresh.*) As far as I . . .

LEDA: (*Imitating Henry, to the old man.*) For illegal possession. (*To Henry.*) As far as my . . .

FRANKIE: Serves her right. Dragging those pictures all over the place. I had a sister, her name was Frances, she always said . . .

BREEZE: (*Turning away from him.*) At least he understood what this is all about. I . . .

LEDA: That shouldn't be too hard to guess, I s'ppose, with a fire like that. My . . .

FRANÇOIS FANT: (*At the stand with the mirrors.*) Fantastic, wouldn't you say?

BARKER: Terrific, ladies and gentlemen, just terrific, absolutely terrific! Every ball a hit. Every ball a punch in your own face!

FANT: What's going on in front? Where are the mirrors? There are no more mirrors. I think that's outrageous. What's going on here? Will you hurry up and get us some more mirrors. Am I supposed to throw my ball up in the air? Ah, here come mine, finally! Impressive, aren't they?

MME. FANT: (*From the back.*) My child, I implore you, don't do it, please, my child!

FANT: Good God, all I need is for that old bitch to show up here! (*He aims.*)

MME. FANT: My child, there you are, my one and only, dearly beloved child, I implore you, don't do it, please, my child!

FANT: What do you want, Madame? You are disturbing.

MME. FANT: What are you doing, my child? That's no way to work. Believe me, please, believe me, oh my child, how am I supposed to do my work, day and night, night and day, day and night!

FANT: Watch it. I'm ready to shoot.

MME. FANT: Don't! My mirrors! My mirrors! You can't! (*She grabs him by the arm.*)

FANT: (*Tears himself away.*) How dare you? Don't you dare touch me! You must be out of . . .

MME. FANT: (*Throws herself between the mirrors and her son.*) Over my dead body!

FANT: (*Bombarding his mother with balls.*) Would somebody get rid of that person! How can I look at myself? She is in my way!

BARKER: Away, away, away, out of the way, ladies and gentlemen, and we, yes we, and we, that's the place to shoot, that's the place to aim, that's the place to shoot and if you don't get out of the way, you'll die a double death. And we, yes we, and we, ladies and gentlemen, now we . . .

KILLOFF: Has anyone seen the photographer? I mean, really! I'm looking for the photographer. Let me tell you, there's a photographer still on the loose. Showing himself in public! That takes some guts! That must be stopped at once, he and his filthy pursuits. D'you know the photographer? That's the one with the car.

SHAKEE: Th-that's not a he, i-it's a she. I arrested her m-myself.

KILLOFF: You don't say! He had the nerve to disguise himself! I mean she. Some maniac! Very dangerous, I'd say. And she talked like a man. I could have sworn it was a man.

SHAKEE: She w-was w-wearing a gray w-wig and sh-she k-kept looking for something on the f-floor.

KILLOFF: That's right. That's her.

SHAKEE: C-caught red-handed.

KILLOFF: So it was a woman. Well, of course, that's why she wanted to marry me.

SHAKEE: R-remember this for your t-testimony.

KILLOFF: Boy oh boy, is she going to get it! She'll hear a testimony she won't believe! I mean, really!

(*A voice from afar: "I am a sow! I am a sow!"*)

BARASS: (*At the fire.*) Damn heat! I'm tellin' you, some kind o' heat! I'm gonna get real mad in that damn heat.

ANNA: Now you're gonna get mad because of the heat?!

BARASS: I'm gonna get mad, 'cause I like gettin' mad.

ANNA: C'mon, you've got nothing left to throw in anyway.

BARASS: (*Points to the baby carriage nearby.*) She's got somethin' in that carriage. That's gotta burn.

ANNA: C'mon, you're not gonna take somebody's baby carriage. You can't do that!

BARASS: Dummy! There ain't no child in that carriage right next to the fire. That carriage is loaded with stuff for burning. Everything's for burning. And who's gonna burn it? Me! You—you go, you hear me!

HOLY: That shouldn't be too hard. I'll go get it right away.

(*A voice from afar: "I am a sow! I am a sow!"*)

KALDAUN JUNIOR: Fy-aaahhh! Fy-aaahhh- Fy-ah!

MAY: But it's screaming!

LUISE: I think that's coming from the opposite direction.

HOLY: I can't hear no baby! Miss Bonnie May's always got babies on her mind.

LUISE: I wonder why.

MAY: But I heard it.

(*The voice from afar: "I am a sow! I am a sow!"*)

HOLY: I can't hear no baby. A man is always right. (*She approaches the carriage. Marie blocks her way.*) Lemme have it.

MARIE: (*Silent.*)

HOLY: Lemme have it. He's waiting.

MARIE: (*Silent.*)

HOLY: I don't want it for myself. Can't you see him over there?

LYA KALDAUN: (*Standing next to them.*) Eugene, what do you think, shall I throw it now?

EUGENE KALDAUN: Hold off a bit. Simple as that.

HOLY: You keep lookin' in the wrong direction, I mean that handsome fella over there. C'mon now, lemme have it!

LYA: I'm holding it in my hand, Eugene. What do you say?

EUGENE: You throw it right in. But take your time. Simple as that.

HOLY: Jesus, how stupid can you get! Don't you understand! Well, then you're gonna get it! Lemme have it right now. (*She pushes Marie out of the way.*)

MARIE: (*Hissing.*) Nothing I give you, just so you know, nothing!

KALDUAN JUNIOR: (*Heartbreakingly.*) Fy-ahh-yah-yah-yah! Fy-ah-yah-yah-yah!

HOLY: (*Recoils.*)

LYA: Eugene, I'm ready!

EUGENE: Alright. Go ahead then! (*Lya throws the mirror in the fire.*)

HOLY: (*Spits.*) That is disgusting! Leaving a baby, an infant, right next to such a big fire! That is really disgusting. I'd like to see the parents of that poor child!

VOICE FROM AFAR: I am a sow! I am a sow!

ANNA: C'mon, you're not gonna undress now because of that heat! All we need is for you to undress!

BARASS: You bet I will. My new jacket's all sweaty already.

ANNA: You see, you should've brought your old one.

MAY: The things a man can eat!

LUISE: My air force commander was always starving too. Whenever he was affectionate, he was also hungry.

MAY: He's got to eat to stay in shape.

LUISE: Oh my God, he's taking off his clothes.

MAY: He's taking off his clothes.

LUISE: He can get away with it. He's a man, mind you.

MAY: Just like Mariano Bello before the car accident.

ANNA: Now you did it! So, now, everybody thinks you like running around naked!

HOLY: (*Empty-handed.*) It's not my fault. Disgusting! Leaving an infant right next to an open fire! That is really disgusting!

THERESA SHRIEK: (*Leaps toward the fire, screaming at the top of her lungs. While she is running, she is tearing her clothes off her body.*) I am a sow! I am a sow!

MILLI: (*Right behind her.*) Mama! For God's sake! Mama's gonna throw herself in the fire!

THERESA: I am a sow! I am a sow!

MILLI: Hurry up, Freddy! Mama's gonna throw herself in the fire! Don't just stand there. Hurry!

HERO: Now, now, let's not cry "Wolf" too soon.

HOLY: I'll be damned, she's really gonna do it!

LUISE: She's going to jump into the fire! God in heaven, have mercy on us!

THERESA: I am a sow! I am a sow!

MAY: A noble spirit, a ready heart.

MILLI: Freddy! My mother! My mother!

BARASS: Make room for the lifesaver, everybody.

THERESA: I am a sow! I am a sow!

(*People are gathering from all sides. In the tremendous noise one can discern only the voice of Theresa Shriek. It has gotten dark and the fire is very bright. As the curtain is coming down, one can hear the Barker, his voice slowly rising and slowly fading:*)

BARKER: Now we, and we, and we, ladies and gentleman, yes we!

PART II

One side of a street

Some low houses to the left and right. A second street, coming from far away, ends up in the center. Every house has its own special color. Wild mixtures of thousands of songs are moving down each street. They merge at the intersection where they form a two-part static block of noise. There is no one in the streets. One can't tell who is singing. Suddenly all the windows of all the houses fly open. A head appears in every window. They all scream in unison: QUIET! The windows are being slammed. As soon as the heads have disappeared, the singing starts all over again, only much stronger than before. Apparently, every one of these people has his own special song, which he practices as vigorously as possible. Instruments don't seem to be popular around here, where only voices can be heard. After a while, the windows fly open again, this time more vehemently than before. The heads are no longer in agreement:

Quiet!
Out of key!
Out of key!
You're singing out of key!
Quiet!
Would you close your window!
Silence! You're disturbing me!
You're disturbing me!

Shut up!
Quiet!

(*Some are singing again, while others are still cursing. The windows open and close repeatedly, in shorter and shorter, ever more frantic intervals. Soon everybody is cursing and singing in a wild confusion of noises and sounds.*)

Living Room
(*Widow Holy, Miss Bonnie May and Nurse Luise*)

HOLY: His heart's fine. In the ten years I've been living with him, he's never had problems with his heart. He's doing fine. He's gonna be living for a long time. Not like my first husband, bless his soul. He was gone in no time. Two months in seventh heaven and gone he was!

MAY: I have the feeling he'll kill himself pretty soon.

HOLY: Barass! C'mon, you've gotta be outa' your mind. As long as he loves me, he's gonna stay alive. He said so himself.

LUISE: Not that I mind. But how long will he be able to get away with it? I mean . . . with his first wife right here in the house?

HOLY: He needs her to fight with. That's what he said. I'm happy she's here. If she wasn't around, who'd have to take his crap? Me!

MAY: Men are so edgy nowadays. Well—the old days . . .

LUISE: Mind you, my Joseph's a gentleman. I have to call him "Director" even at home.

HOLY: When Barass gets stark raving mad I only have to say to him: Barass, show me what you can do and he'll take off his clothes right away and beat his fists against the wall. It's a miracle this house hasn't collapsed yet. (*Proudly.*) We got our eviction notice yesterday.

MAY: Here too? So where d'you want to go now?

HOLY: He's got so much strength. None of us can keep up with him.

MAY: (*Looks around cautiously and giggles.*) The weaker sex, oh dear.

HOLY: Are you startin' again!

LUISE: Mind you, my Joseph's rolling in money. He's earned his title. And I can't complain about the house. It's just like in the hospital, with all the nursing he requires. He's got such unbelievable ideas. A whole ward full of patients doesn't present as many problems. A gentleman. Love repels him. He didn't get married to make love, he says.

MAY: Seems neither of you's happy (*giggling*) the way it's supposed to be according to the song.

HOLY: Miss Bonnie May won't stop until she's got us all behind bars.

BLEISS: (*A peddler, appears in the door, carrying his display case.*) Excuse the disruption, ladies. Do you ladies need anything? Pretty soaps? Pretty stockings? Pretty ribbons for your pretty bosoms?

HOLY: How on earth did you get in?

BLEISS: Through the door, ladies. Just take a look, ladies. No obligation to buy.

HOLY: You won't have much luck here, mister. There's never a penny in this house. Never, ever!

LUISE: I don't mind looking. I might even buy something.

MAY: The things a man can carry!

BLEISS: Help yourselves, ladies. Help yourself to some happiness, ladies, but don't get too greedy now. One moment, please. Now, what have I got here? (*Something flashes in his hand. The ladies screech.*)

HOLY: That's disgusting!

MAY: A sweet secret!

LUISE: Lord Almighty, have mercy on us!

BLEISS: No need to get scared, ladies. It'll pass. Just two minutes, ladies, and it'll all be over again. The price is ridiculous: Five shillings per person. That's unheard of. You show me, ladies, where else you can find that.

(*The women become very agitated. Miss May starts adjusting her blouse. Nurse Luise's head begins to twitch. Widow Holy suddenly grabs the tiny round mirror, which S. Bleiss has been holding up to the ladies, ever so temptingly but with the backside facing them.*)

HOLY: Lemme have it!

MAY: (*As she's adjusting her blouse.*) A sweet secret.

LUISE: And out of the blue! Like an apparition.

BLEISS: May I ask for the remittance.

(*Clumsily, Widow Holy is running for money. Nurse Luise gets her bag. Miss Bonnie May carries her money in her blouse.*)

HOLY: Where did I put my money? I still had some left. My last money, where did I put it?

BLEISS: You'll find it, lady. Wherever I go the ladies would always find a last penny somewhere in the house. It is absolutely impossible that a lady doesn't have any money left for me.

LUISE: I know very well where I keep my money. Just out of the blue!

MAY: I'm ready! I'm ready!

BLEISS: (*Takes the bill she hands him.*) Thank you, lady. Permit me to look at my watch. At exactly 4:24 your face will be revealed.

LUISE: Mind you, I'm next! There's your money!

BLEISS: Thank you, lady. One moment please. Get ready, set: 4:24 P.M. (*He holds the tiny mirror to Bonnie May's face.*)

HOLY: (*Angrily.*) I can't find it. I can't find it. He's stolen it again. Boy, is he gonna get it! Luise honey, can you lend it to me?

LUISE: Shh. Quiet. She's looking!

(There is a penetrating silence. Suddenly one can hear voices from outside.)

BARASS: And me? How about me? Am I nothing?

ANNA: C'mon now, you ain't trying to tell me that you are somebody.

BARASS: I am a free man. I can do whatever I want. I can do with myself whatever I want. That's how it is. Why d'you keep runnin' after me?

ANNA: C'mon now, you ain't trying to tell me that I'm running after you.

BARASS: That's the second time that you come runnin' after me today.

ANNA: If you would have stayed at home, I wouldn't've come after you. So there.

BARASS: How'd you know where I'm going? You don't understand a thing. Stupid bitch!

ANNA: You said yourself that you had no money.

BARASS: What I do with my money is none of your goddam business!

ANNA: C'mon now, you don't wanna tell me that you suddenly got money.

HOLY: Sure. 'Cause he stole it again. He stole it from me.

LUISE: *(Imploring her.)* Shh! She's almost done.

(Widow Holy leaves the room.)

BLEISS: Get ready: 4:26 P.M.

MAY: Just a moment. Just a moment.

LUISE: Mind you, I've been waiting for a long time. My Joseph's waiting too. I can't afford to wait that long.

BLEISS: *(To Bonnie May.)* Sorry, lady. But the other lady has paid too.

MAY: I just want to quickly take off my blouse. *(Whining.)* Half a minute! A quarter minute!

BLEISS: I'm sorry, lady.

MAY: I'll pay again. I've got enough. I'll pay. Here's the money.

LUISE: What about me? I want my money back!

BLEISS: Lady number 1 takes off her blouse while lady number 2 is looking. When the second lady's done looking, it's the first lady's second turn. A Solomonic decision, ladies.

MAY: *(Sobbing.)* But I want to look now. I don't want to interrupt . . .

LUISE: *(Hissing.)* Who brought the mir- . . . ? Would you mind leaving the Solomonic decision up to this gentleman? He is the owner!

BLEISS: Ready, lady! It is 4:27. *(Flashes the mirror in front of Nurse Luise.)*

HOLY: *(Drags in Barass. Anna meakly behind them.)* You dirty thief, you! You stole it again! Thief! I had it in my sewing basket!

ANNA: So—there. You stole it.

BARASS: That ain't stealing. That woman's my wife. I took it.

LUISE: *(Without turning her rigid gaze away from the mirror, as though praying.)* Quiet, please. Please be quiet. I can't. Please. How am I . . .

(*May is standing to the side, she is fighting with her blouse. She can't be bothered by Barass's entrance.*)

BARASS: So that's what it is. That gangster's peddling a shard! That's why she needs the money! Wouldn't you like that! Stupid bitches! What d'ya think you're doin'? In my house! I'll report you! I'll report all of you! (*He snatches the mirror from Bleiss. With his other hand he punches his face with terrible force.*)

LUISE: (*As if intoxicated.*) I am—not done—yet.

BARASS: You ain't done yet, goddam sow! In my house! I'll report you all! They're gonna get that bastard!

ANNA: I wasn't here. I didn't bring him here. If you wouldn't have gone out, I wouldn't have either. I'd have thrown him out right away. He wouldn't've made it through the door. (*She approaches Barass's hand.*)

BARASS: So, you wanna split, huh! (*He grabs Bleiss at the collar.*) While I still got those two chicks in the house!

ANNA: You see—I told 'em to leave. Didn't I tell 'em to leave!

BLEISS: Sir, have mercy. I have eight children at home, sir, eight mouths, eight hungry mouths to feed, the wife on her deathbed for thirty years now, sir. Have pity on the wife, the children, sir.

BARASS: Why don't you get a regular job, filthy bastard! I've gotta work too. Me! I'm a special man and I've gotta work. I've got two wives and I've got two children too. You think they come free, you filthy bastard?

BLEISS: I've gotta work, sir. If you'd only know I've gotta work day and night, sir, and the beating I get everywhere. Why? Because I bring some pleasure to the people. Do I get any pleasure out of it? Oh no! A penniless peddler in the worst of poverty, sir. At home the most terrible cold, not a crust of bread in the house and the beating I get everywhere. But I've never ever been reported, sir. How can we do this to him, that's what people say to themselves. The death penalty, a father of eight, a dying wife, sir. (*He kneels and clasps his hands.*)

BARASS: (*Lets go of him.*) But I'll break your damn shard, you dog! I'll break it into a thousand pieces. Then you can try and find yourself another shard. (*He lifts his hand which is holding the mirror. The four women scream.*)

ANNA: For God's sake. That precious shard!

HOLY: That's disgusting! How stupid can you get!

LUISE: Lord Almighty, have mercy on us!

MAY: Crazy! Just crazy!

(*Shrieking and moaning they approach Barass. S. Bleiss disappears as quickly as he can.*)

BARASS: You like that, don't you, that shard? I'm still gonna smash it. The forbidden fruit. Oh yes! Typical! Stupid broads! Wouldn't you like that, they find a shard in my house and I get sentenced to death.

HOLY: You could lemme have one look at least.

ANNA: You can sell it. They go for five thousand apiece.

LUISE: Mind you, there'll still be time to break it.

MAY: And I was all set!

BARASS: I'm still gonna break it! I'm gonna scare the hell out of you, stupid broads!

(He hurls the mirror to the floor. The women throw themselves on it. He separates the huddle and picks up the shard. It is still in one piece. Barass laughs wildly.)

BARASS: You didn't know that, my little chickies, did ya! It's unbreakable. It's made of metal. Plain metal! Tomorrow morning it's gotta be out of here. Now I've got enough of your women's business. *(To Anna.)* You go cook! *(To Widow Holy.)* You go with your girl friends, that's good manners. You bring the girls home. They'll be scared, all alone, out there in the street. I'm staying. I'm not gonna go out anymore.

ANNA: There—you see. You should've stayed home to begin with! *(She goes to cook.)*

HOLY: I'll be right back.

LUISE: Do we really have to leave right away? I wouldn't mind staying another half hour.

BARASS: I want my peace now. I'm fed up with broads.

MAY: The things a man needs! We could starve to death right next to him!

THE STREET CORNER

(Frankie Nada stands on the street corner to the left, he is ten years older, bent even lower, as if in the last ten years he had been carrying heavier loads than in the seventy previous ones. François Fant strolls in casually from the left. Nada immediately "attacks" him, without actually leaving his spot.)

NADA: Oh my God, it's you, sir, don't you look gorgeous!

(Fant doesn't look.)

NADA: Sir, gorgeous, sir! I haven't seen you in such a long time!

(Fant gives the old man a quick, scornful look.)

NADA: Don't you recognize me, sir, gorgeous sir? Oh well, an old ugly stupid fool like me! How could you recognize me? But I recognized you right away: that's my gorgeous young gentleman!

FANT: What's going on? How come? What are you talking about?

NADA: I recognized you right away. You look even more gorgeous now. Jesus help me, so gorgeous! Unbelievably gorgeous!

FANT: How come? What do you mean?

NADA: I'm just sayin'. I mean, sir, gorgeous sir, I've know you such a long time, sir. And I always think, now, that's as gorgeous as he'll ever get. There's a limit even to his beauty and this makes me very sad.

FANT: How dare you? Old fool!

NADA: That's what I mean! That's what I mean, sir, gorgeous sir! Don't misunderstand me, an old fool like me, dumb and ugly as I am! I mean every time I see you sir, gorgeous sir, you've become more gorgeous yet! And I quietly say to myself: Is this really the same person? Is it possible? Is he for real? Of course, I say to myself, it's him. It can only be him, 'cause such beauty (*sings*), "That's once in a lifetime, it won't happen again, dear."

FANT: What do you want?

NADA: Nothing, sir, God forbid, gorgeous sir! I want nothing, absolutely nothing! I'm happy, that's all, stupid, ugly old me, standing here and suddenly I see this beautiful young gentleman. What a pleasure! I could cry for joy. What beauty! Makes me want to sing and dance and shout with happiness! Yoo-peeehhh!

FANT: You?? How??

NADA: Right you are, sir, gorgeous sir. Get angry with me. Old cripple that I am, standing around all day, good for nothing, stupid ugly old me.

FANT: Is this your spot?

NADA: With your permission, sir, gorgeous sir. It's been such a long time, since I've last seen you. It actually made me homesick, my heart was filled with such great longing. You're gonna die, I thought, without ever seeing him again. My beautiful young gentleman.

FANT: When was the last time I came by?

NADA: Oh sir, gorgeous sir, it's been such a long time! It's been exactly eight horrible days.

FANT: There! (*Hands him a coin.*) But don't you dare peddle your flatteries again. You understand! (*He strolls on.*)

(*Lya Kaldaun enters right, loaded with packages. Fritz Hero behind her, continuously raising his hat with great flair.*)

HERO: Madam, permit me to thank you from the bottom of my heart!

LYA: How dare you!

HERO: The male species is forever indebted to you. Am I the only one? I am not, as you can see for yourself. Everyone is running after you.

LYA: Would you please leave me alone!

HERO: If only I could, madam, I'd give anything to be able to leave you alone. It's impossible.

LYA: In the middle of the street. You scare me.

HERO: Pardon me, madam, but I know no fear. I lay down my heart at the feet of a beautiful lady!

LYA: I am married.

HERO: If I may say so, I don't mind. A beautiful lady is like the sun. Doesn't the sun shine for every man?

LYA: Every man! Really? Is that what you think? I won't have it!

HERO: I say Everyman meaning myself. I am not Everyman. I am Chairman of the Four!

(To the left, Wenzel Wondrak passes Nada very quickly.)

NADA: Oh my God, it's you sir, don't you look gorgeous!

WONDRAK: Shut up. *(Turns into the side street.)*

NADA: Bad mood. Hasn't had his dinner.

LYA: That's what I thought.

HERO: I am no spendthrift. Even the Chairman of the Four appreciates the value of money. But life has its priorities, pretty lady. For a lady, I'd sacrifice the last thing I own. I've loved many ladies. As a matter of principle, I only fall in love with ladies of the upper class.

LYA: Are you serious?

HERO: Absolutely. May I tell you a riddle, pretty lady?

LYA: Yes, but hurry, I'm almost home.

HERO: Who has eyes like stars, a rose of a mouth and hair as black as an Arabian night? Take a guess, pretty lady and make a man's heart jump for joy.

LYA: I don't get it.

HERO: The prize-winning answer is a song: "You, you, yes only you."

LYA: I get it.

HERO: May I kindly ask you for a favor, pretty lady?

LYA: It depends . . .

HERO: That song isn't mine, pretty lady. I'm just singing it, because it's part of the riddle.

LYA: What's your song?

HERO: I won't tell you now. I'd rather save it as my farewell gift.

LYA: I'm afraid that won't be possible. If my husband should see you!

HERO: Don't you worry, pretty lady. Times change, as they say and my time is yet to come. And I shall give you—well, guess what!

LYA: I'd love to, but . . .

HERO: I shall give you . . . my photograph.

LYA: *(Shrieks.)* That's not possible!

HERO: Madam, everything is possible with me. You don't believe me? I don't blame you. That's the way men are. They promise you the world and don't keep their word. But you shall see with your own starry eyes. Permit me, madam. *(He hands her a picture.)* Careful! We are being watched!

LYA: What can I say! It's you. A rarity!

HERO: That's me.

LYA: I can't get enough of it!

HERO: As I said, for a lady, I'd sacrifice the last thing I own. May I?

LYA: Pity. Really. What a pity. (*She hands him back his picture.*)

HERO: One day, you shall own this picture, pretty lady.

LYA: You're precious. I'm almost home. Until tomorrow then.

HERO: Same time. In front of the same store. I can't wait.

LYA: You'll bring it . . . your picture.

HERO: If you wish, pretty lady.

LYA: I'll see you!

HERO: (*Sings, raising his hat.*) I'm kissing your hand, madam.

NADA: Oh my God, it's you, madam. Don't you look gorgeous. So young, so beautiful. I haven't seen you in such a long time.

(*Lya passes him without paying attention. Killoff enters left, in dignified and elaborate garb.*)

NADA: Oh my God, it's you, sir! Don't you look gorgeous. I haven't seen you in such a long time. Sir, gorgeous . . .

KILLOFF: (*Turns toward Nada and looks him straight in the face.*) You just wait, buddy!

(*He walks on. He has reached the right edge of the stage when Nurse Luise appears on the left. She carries a man's coat and a muffler on her arm and holds a hat and cane in her hand. Killoff stops, so does Nurse Luise. She waits. He waves to her, nonchalantly. She rushes toward him.*)

LUISE: You want to do it now?

KILLOFF: Who's going to stop me? There's no law against changing your clothes!

LUISE: But mind you, you might catch a cold. That's the last thing we'd need . . . a cold. (*She helps him change his clothes.*)

KILLOFF: Nothing can happen if you do it right. You just have to do it right. Right? Right!

LUSIE: I'll try my best.

KILLOFF: Easy, easy! That hurts. I'm not a rag doll. I'm human. I mean, really!

LUISE: Please forgive me, Joseph. It won't happen again.

KILLOFF: Irresponsible, I find it quite irresponsible. Really!

LUISE: I'll try my best. It won't happen again. Please forgive me, Joseph!

KILLOFF: So. There. I dare anyone to stop me now!

LUISE: May I ask, which way are we going?

KILLOFF: Back, of course. Always those dumb questions.

LUISE: I'm sorry, I just wasn't so sure today.

KILLOFF: That's just what I like! Now, don't you forget anything, you hear!

Well, I'm on my way.

(*Nurse Luise stays behind with the coat, muffler and hat, which Killoff had worn before. He walks back to Nada and slowly turns once all the way around.*)

NADA: Oh my God, it's you, sir! Don't you look gorgeous! More gorgeous, more youthful than ever. It's a miracle, really! Almost beyond recognition. Such youth! Such beauty! A miracle.

(*Killoff nods and exits.*)

LUISE: (*Follows. She hands Nada a coin.*) That's from my husband.

BONNIE MAY'S LIVE-IN KITCHEN

(*Wenzel Wondrak at the table, Bonnie May at the stove.*)

WONDRAK: Where's my food? I'm in a hurry.

MAY: It's coming. It's coming.

WONDRAK: It's coming, ladies and gentlemen, it's coming, it's coming in a jiffy or else you'll have it coming and it won't be funny.

MAY: It'll be yummy yummy!

WONDRAK: I'm waiting.

MAY: I'm coming. I'm coming.

WONDRAK: (*Examines what she is putting on the table.*) No need to make such a big deal over that crap. Where the hell's the wine?

MAY: Shall I get you a jug? I'm going. I'll be right back. (*Exits warbling.*) "For you, my love . . ."

WONDRAK: But hurry, will ya! And watch it, ya hear, don't break your fat old legs or you'll have to lick the wine from the floor. 'Cause I, I don't drink off the floor! Only out of a glass, ladies and gentlemen, only out of a glass, the forbidden glass, whch isn't a glass (*he lifts up the cup which is made of unglazed clay*). Then what—what, what, what on earth is this?—This is the earth, the clay, the crap. (*He vehemently throws the cup to the floor*) from which our Lord made man. (*He sings.*) Watch out world, here I come, yes I, I, I. (*He eats and hollers between each bite.*) I! I! I!

MAY: (*Breathlessly.*) I'm back! I'm back!

WONDRAK: Gimme the wine!

MAY: (*Sings.*) For you, my love, I got all dressed up . . .

WONDRAK: I'm done eatin' and now I'm gonna do you in. Watch out world, here I come!

MAY: You look just like him. Especially when you're singing. Gorgeous body and fire in the eyes . . .

WONDRAK: Watch how you talk to me. No intimacies, please. Show some re-

spect, will you! Will you, will you, show me, show me your, show me your
. . . respect, I say. That's it.

MAY: You must eat some more. A man must eat or he ain't no good.

WONDRAK: All right then, gimme some more. I'll stay as long as I feel like eating.

MAY: I've plenty more. Just a second, just a second. (*She goes to the stove, warbling.*) For you, my love . . .

WONDRAK: Crazy old pig, with her 150 years!

MAY: Here I come!

WONDRAK: All right, I'm gonna eat this. But if you had anything else in
mind, you better forget it, yes, ladies and gentlemen, I say, you better forget it.

MAY: Mr. Wondrak, please! What makes you think I'd think of such a thing.
I only invited you 'cause I knew it was really you. (*She giggles and whispers in his ear.*)

WONDRAK: I know. I know I'm incognito. I know who I am when I'm incognito. And what became of me? A concierge. A mysterious concierge.

MAY: But legal, nonetheless. Don't you forget it, legal, nonetheless.

WONDRAK: Absolutely. Absolutely.

MAY: Now upstairs, at Barass's? You know the man, my poor friend Holy
moved in with. Something's fishy. I know it, I was there. This bastard
came and tried to trick us. We girls screamed: Police! That's when Barass
came home and right away he kept it for himself.

WONDRAK: (*Jumps up, screaming.*) What? They've got a shard upstairs? And
you're telling me now?! Boy, are you gonna get it! (*He rushes out.*)

MAY: Now that woman's goin' to jail with that Barass. Birds of a feather . . .
Serves her right! She's destroyed a marriage. "For you, my love . . ."

THE KALDAUNS' BEDROOM

LYA: Eugene, what shall I wear today?

EUGENE: That dickey's too stiff again! Too much starch! For the hundredth
time.

LYA: Eugene, what shall I wear today?

EUGENE: I don't have to put up with this. Simple as that. I can do without my
dickey. I can do without it. Very simple, I just won't go out. So. There.

LYA: Eugene, what do you think I should wear today? I could wear the brown
dress, but I don't like the sleeves. They make me look like . . . what do you
always say they make me look like, Eugene?

EUGENE: I don't have the skin of an elephant! I can feel it. Stiff, yes, but that
stiff? No. That really is the end of it. Simple as that.

LYA: Now this woman got a spot on my brown dress. What shall I do? A spot
on my brown dress. Eugene, I can't wear my brown dress.

EUGENE: Very simple. We'll just put the shirt back where it was. Where does it go? Nobody cares. Oh well. We'll just put it here and I won't go out. So. There.

LYA: What am I going to wear? That woman better not show her face. I'd scratch her eyes out. I am speechless. Eugene, there's a spot on my brown dress. What shall I wear today?

EUGENE: (*Sits down in a chair, puts his hands in his lap and stares straight ahead while she is talking. As soon as she is finished, he jumps up.*) I am saying it for the last time: I am not going out. So. There.

LYA: Shall I wear the brown dress anyway? Eugene, would you take a look at that spot? If you'd only take a look! Shall I? Maybe it's not all that bad.

EUGENE: (*Sings.*) "Baby you dance just like my wife!" Those oldies are still my favorites. Simple as that. The way we used to glide over the glistening dance floors. (*He startles and looks around.*) Who's listening at the door again?

MARIE: (*Enters. She delivers her lines alternatingly to the left and the right side.*) I did not make spot. Dickey is exactly so stiff like sir wanted it. There can be no spot. Sir himself felt dickey and felt fine. Madam tried dress before and where was spot then? Permit me—sir, I touch dickey! Lady will be astonished! One, two, three, spot disappears. I have two very good ears on my head. In old days, I had my peace, there were mirrors still.

LYA: Marie, I am speechless! What did I tell you? You must not use dirty words. If the children should hear you! I won't have it!

EUGENE: You can't do it. Simple as that. Marie, I am telling you for the last time, I won't put up with it.

LYA: What more do I have to tell you? My husband had the final word. The children must not hear any dirty words.

MARIE: What? In old days we had mirrors and nobody got upset.

LYA: Marie, my husband has told you for the last time. Very simple. He won't put up with it.

EUGENE: Marie, what shall I tell you? I am speechless. I won't have it.

MARIE: Is there spot? No spot. And dickey is exactly right. Enough nagging. And me, always listen, ashamed. I quit. Madam, sir, I tell you. I go! (*At the top of her lungs.*) Mirror! Mirror! Mirror! (*She runs off.*)

EUGENE AND LYA: Do we need this?

EUGENE: You and your spot? Always the same. I won't listen all the same. What makes you think I care about your spot? I know there is no spot. I simply ignore you when you start lying.

LYA: Eugene, what do you want me to say? Your dickey's exquisite. It never felt so good. I could wear it myself. And you will have to admit that I have delicate breasts. Eugene, I'm asking you, am I right or not?

EUGENE: Of course, when you talk to me like this. That's what I've been waiting for. You have to care, that's all. You think the dickey's all right? Why don't you touch it one more time? Simple as that. If you think so, I'll wear it, just like it is.

LYA: I am speechless. It never felt so good. In all the years we've been married, that's the best it's ever been. It even gives you a touch of class. I'm for the brown dress, what do you think?

EUGENE: Then I'll wear it. I listen to you. Because it's you. Simple as that. So you think it's that good today! You say it gives me class? Tell me more.

LYA: What can I tell you, Eugene? I better get ready. We'll be late again. I'll stay with the brown dress, what do you say?

EUGENE: That you find it that good today . . . I didn't really think it was all that bad. But that good?! You are an adventurous woman. Simple as that. Adventurous. Always full of surprises, nobody knows what's going to happen—the suspense is thrilling, simply thrilling.

LYA: Eugene, darling, are you really talking to me? How do you say I am? Adventuresome? Eugene, oh, Eugene, adventuresome . . . me?! I keep you in suspense? I am speechless. You're thrilled? Eugene, my darling, my baby, oh honey, the brown dress it'll be.

EUGENE: Very simple.

KALDAUN'S SECOND CHILD: (*A short and very ugly little girl comes running in.*) Mommy, daddy, mommy, daddy! What's a mirror? I wanna know, what's a mirror? Please! I want a mirror. Marie says mirror. I want a mirror too. Mommy, daddy, is it pretty, a mirror? What's a mirror? Please! I wanna know! Pretty please!!

PARENTS: (*Stop their dressing and scream at top of their lungs.*) Yukki! Yukki! Yukki! (*The little girl gets slapped on the mouth.*)

THE STREET

(*Hansi, Puppi, Gretl, Lizzi, Heidi and Lori—six young girls around 18—are coming down the street, cheerful, loud, and giggling a lot.*)

LORI: Puppi, now do it with me!

PUPPI: You're too tall for me!

LORI: You can stand on that rock.

PUPPI: I'll fall down.

LORI: I'll hold you.

PUPPI: How long?

LORI: Forever!

PUPPI: And suddenly you'll let go of me.

LORI: Never!

PUPPI: You always say that.

LORI: I promise! Cross my heart.

LIZZI: (*To Puppi.*) Don't believe her. She'll trick you again.

LORI: Puppi! Come on now!!

PUPPI: You're the tallest and I'm the shortest. We don't match at all.

LORI: That doesn't matter. Yours are so nice and gray.

LIZZI: (*To Lori.*) Leave her alone, if she doesn't want to.

LORI: (*To Lizzi.*) I don't like you. You've got charcoals!

LIZZI: I wouldn't let you anyway. So you might as well forget it!

LORI: Come on, Puppi! Afterwards I'll tell you something. Only you.

PUPPI: All right then, but not for long.

(*She steps on the rock. Lori comes very close and holds her by the arms.*)

LORI: You got your balance?

PUPPI: Yes, but don't let go.

(*They keep looking into each other's eyes for a long time.*)

LIZZI: Look, Hansi, Lori really likes her new dress.

HANSI: It's got a nice color.

LIZZI: She keeps looking at herself forever.

HANSI: Puppi's got just the right eyes for it. Nice and gray.

LIZZI: That dress doesn't even go with gray. Lori's got no taste.

HANSI: You just don't like her. Did you go fishing again?

LIZZI: Yes, yesterday. But it was the last time, my father said.

HANSI: Really. Why? Your father loves to go fishing, doesn't he?

GRETL: Didn't you hear? All the fish died.

(*Laughter.*)

LIZZI: The guard's really getting pushy. You can hardly move anymore. He's watching like crazy. Yesterday, he gave my father a ticket.

HANSI: Really? What for?

LIZZI: He opened his eyes too soon. And when he opened them, there was no fish. That's what the guard says. But my father did feel a fish pulling on the line or he wouldn't have opened his eyes. The fish got off that's all, it can happen, my father says. He would have to be crazy to open his eyes if he knew there was no fish on the hook. Why would he want to act against the law? He is a decent man and he has proved it. He did get a permit and he signed it and he has always stuck to its rules. Still, the guard keeps after him. A real nasty guy!

GRETL: Why do you need a permit to go fishing?

HANSI: That's what I want to know.

LIZZI: You don't know? Oh well, of course you never went fishing. Without a permit you can't join the fisherman's club. And that costs a lot of money. Fishing costs me a fortune, my father says.

GRETL: So what does the permit say?

LIZZI: The permit says what you have to do when you go fishing. Your eyes have to be closed. You may open them only when you feel a fish pulling on the line. Or you can stand with your back turned to the water. Then you can keep your eyes open. You may look at the fish only from afar. The club provides a private guard who's very nice. But besides him there's also a government guard, just to make sure. And he's really nasty.

GRETL: Who'd want to go fishing if it's such a bore!

LIZZI: That's why we aren't going anymore. That was the last time, my father . . .

HANSI: I would've thought fishing's more fun. I thought you'd sit there looking in the water.

LIZZI: What do you know! But of course that's because you never went fishing.

HEIDI: A fish's so nice and smooth. Like metal used to be . . . in the old days. There was a time when metals were nice and smooth and shiny.

GRETL: Yes and people were allowed to go swimming in those days. Those were the days.

HANSI: Just look at Lori, will you. She's still at it!

LIZZI: My God, she really likes herself.

HEIDI: I'm goin' to get Puppi. (*She runs back.*)

GRETL: I don't know why everybody's so crazy about Puppi! I want Hansi. (*She links arms with Hansi.*)

HANSI: I'm waiting for Puppi.

LIZZI: I'm waiting for Puppi.

GRETL: Come on, Hansi, you do it with me.

HANSI: It's boring . . . always with you.

GRETL: Boring! Boy, I don't believe you said that.

HANSI: I just don't want to always do it with you.

GRETL: You said I have blue eyes.

HANSI: So what! Lots of people have blue eyes.

GRETL: You said I make you look the prettiest.

HANSI: That's how I always look.

GRETL: You said Puppi makes you look all gray.

HANSI: I just said that because I didn't want to hurt your feelings.

GRETL: You hurt my feelings? You could never hurt my feelings!

HANSI: I don't want to hurt your feelings. But if you really want to know . . .

GRETL: Yes, I do. I really want to know. I have to know why you are so mean to me.

HANSI: Mean! You're mean! Your eyes are too small if you really want to know. D'you really think I can see myself in them? I can't see a thing when I do it with you.

GRETL: I don't even want you. I'd rather have Puppi. Her eyes are much prettier than yours. (*She fights back her tears.*)

HANSI: Good God, now she's gotta cry! That's all we need.

GRETL: I'm not crying. He's crying.

(*A little boy who is crying is crossing the street.*)

HANSI: What's his problem?
LORI: (*Joins them.*) That's Kaldaun Jr.
HANSI: Puppi's free. (*She runs over to Puppi.*)
GRETL: (*Calling after Hansi.*) Never mind. I'm staying with Lori.

(*Hansi has linked arms with Puppi and started a conversation with her. Lizzi and Hansi are fighting vehemently for Puppi. They agree to take turns looking in her eyes, while Heidi is again waiting patiently.*)

LORI: Why is he crying?
GRETL: Go home, kid.
BOY: I don't want to.
LORI: Why are you crying?
BOY: 'Cause I have to.
LORI: That's no reason. You shouldn't be crying.
BOY: But I have to.
LORI: A big boy like you!
GRETL: How old are you?
BOY: I don't know. (*He keeps crying.*)
LORI: But you must know how old you are.
GRETL: Such a big boy.
BOY: I don't know. That's why I'm crying.
LORI: Why don't you ask your mother.
GRETL: Or your father. Then you'll know.
BOY: They won't tell me. That's why I'm crying.
LORI AND GRETL: (*Looking at each other meaningfully.*) Oh!
BOY: D'you think I'm twelve?
LORI: How should we know?
BOY: I mean, do I look like twelve?
LORI: Oh yes. You must be twelve. More than twelve.
BOY: (*To Gretl.*) What d'you think?
GRETL: I'd say fourteen.
LORI: But that's no reason to cry.
BOY: Who's crying?
GRETL: You did. Before.
BOY: (*Grinning.*) I only wanted to know how old I look. (*He runs off with a big grin.*)
GRETL: Boy, he starts early, doesn't he.
LORI: I'd like to know who taught him!

(*Boy turns around at a safe distance and screams "MIRROR" to the girls. Then he takes off as quickly as he can.*)

GRETL: He's got nerve.

LORI: At his age!

(*Puppi and Heidi arrive, arm in arm, flanked by Hansi and Lizzi.*)

PUPPI: François is the best looking man in the world.

HEIDI: Fritz always wears black glasses.

PUPPI: François also has black glasses but he prefers to carry them in his pocket.

HEIDI: Then why have glasses?

PUPPI: He needs them for the meetings. And today I can come with him to the meeting.

GRETL: The meeting? Really? You don't say!

HEIDI: Fritz never lets me. I never know where Fritz has his meetings. They're top secret, he says.

PUPPI: Come on, François always sees Fritz at those meetings. They're going to the same meetings.

HEIDI: That may be. But Fritz is a really special person at those meetings. Not like everyone else. That's why. He always has to wear his glasses. Otherwise, he'd be like everyone else.

PUPPI: Why did they pick Fritz? François is much better looking.

HEIDI: That's a question of character, you know. And Fritz certainly's got character. If I dare call him Fritzl, he won't talk to me for three days. Now he won't even let me call him Fritz. His full name is Friedrich.

PUPPI: You're so lucky he lets you live with him.

HEIDI: That's true. Sometimes he doesn't say a word in eight days. And no one knows why. He doesn't want to see a doctor. He just comes home from school and sits there, staring. He says he's got a headache. And I can't say a word either. If you dare say a single word he goes crazy. He's got character. That's all. If only he wouldn't be so mean sometimes.

PUPPI: What do you want? At least he lets you be with him all the time. I always have to go home. François says . . . here he comes. Bye! Bye! Bye! Bye! Bye! (*Loud, to Fant.*) I can come to the meeting tonight, can't I?

FANT: (*Loud, to her.*) Yes. Unfortunately I've got to go to the meeting tonight.

(*The five girls exit slowly. In the meantime it has become dark. Puppi runs to Fant and tries to kiss him on the mouth. He is looking for something in his pocket.*)

FANT: Wait a minute. Will you wait a minute!

PUPPI: Where did you put it?

FANT: Just wait. It must've slipped into the lining. Too much!

PUPPI: Come on now! You're funny.

FANT: Funny? You call me funny? Never. Things like that can happen.

PUPPI: You could have looked for it before you came.

FANT: That's what I usually do. Too much. Today I had the meeting on my mind, that's why.

PUPPI: You still could have looked for it before.

FANT: Will you stop it now, really! This is unbelievable. I couldn't have left it at home. That never happened to me. (*His movements get more and more fidgety.*)

PUPPI: You know something? We never kissed in the dark. That must feel funny.

FANT: Boring. Why would we want to do that? It makes no sense.

FANT: But what if you can't find the light?

FANT: Stop talking nonsense. Malicious, really.

PUPPI: (*Near tears.*) But if you don't want to kiss me.

FANT: But I want to. I don't believe this . . . Here, I've got it!

PUPPI: Really?

(*He pulls out a flashlight. He pushes the button. It lights up. Puppi grabs him and kisses him on the mouth. He points the light toward her eyes.*)

FANT: Easy does it! I can't see anything.

PUPPI: Wait. One more time.

FANT: It's flickering. Damned. Now I've had it. (*He tears himself away, hurls the flashlight on the floor and tramples on it angrily.*)

PUPPI: What are you doing?

FANT: It's no good. I'm tired of trying to get it to work.

PUPPI: But the case was still good. All it needed was a new battery.

FANT: I can't stand this damn thing anymore. That's the second time it happened to me. It makes me nervous, that's all. Too much, really. I'll tell Maman to get me a new one. Something more sporty.

PUPPI: That's too bad. I just wanted to . . .

FANT: So we'll just have to do without kissing. Big deal. (*He notices Fritz Shakee, who is standing at the corner keeping a close eye on Theresa Shriek's store.*) Anyway, I've got to get to the meeting. Ciao. (*He runs into the store.*)

THERESA SHRIEK'S GENERAL STORE

(*It is small, with low ceilings and dark. On the walls are big white signs with inscriptions lit by special lamps. They stick out as the brightest objects in the store.*)

FLATTERERS DIG THEIR OWN GRAVES
BEWARE OF FLATTERY YE SINFUL KNAVES!
WORK EARNS YOU YOUR DAILY BREAD
FLATTERERS WILL SOON BE DEAD!
FLATTERERS SHOW YOU IN A FALSE LIGHT
THEIR LIES YOU MUST FIGHT! THEIR LIES YOU MUST FIGHT!

THE FLATTERERS KEEP AFTER ME
OH HELP ME LORD I PRAY TO THEE!

(*Theresa Shriek behind the counter. François Fant enters.*)

THERESA: Ah, Monsieur François! What an honor! Of course, the meeting!

FANT: Bonsoir.

THERESA: Monsieur François is first. The other gentlemen aren't here yet.

FANT: How dare you call me Monsieur François, woman! Don't you know my name?

THERESA: Of course I know your name. Monsieur François is the son of Madame Fant. Emily Fant. Madame used to live right on this block. Madame used to shop right in this store. And how is your dear mother? Madame hasn't stepped foot in my store in such a long time.

FANT: Too much work. Much too much.

THERESA: Yeah, she's always been such a hard-working woman.

FANT: Lady. And to you I'm Monsieur Fant, you understand.

THERESA: I knew you, sir, when you were still in diapers.

FANT: I've never been in diapers.

THERESA: When you were just a teeny little boy I meant to say. I don't mean to flatter. I never flatter, never, ever. (*She points to the signs.*) But sir, you were the prettiest, even then. The women would drool after you in the middle of the street. Monsieur was in such demand! Same as today. I wonder where my Millie is.

FANT: Your daughter. I know her too. Pretty. Very pretty, I must say. Could be a beauty if dressed properly, with style, in clothes picked by me.

THERESA: Good God, sir, please don't! Don't commit a flattery. Please don't flatter.

FANT: But she isn't even here. You won't tell her, I hope. Why shouldn't I say that I find your daughter quite special.

THERESA: Special, yes. That's what everybody's saying. (*She sneaks to a door, opens it quickly and peeks into the back room.*) No, she isn't here. Sometimes she sneaks in and listens to what people are saying about her. I've my problems with that girl. Otherwise she's very nice. I just have to keep an eye on her. After all, I can't just hand her over to any Tom, Dick or Harry.

(*Fritz Shakee stalks stiffly through the store. He wears black glasses and doesn't say hello. François Fant and Theresa freeze in their conversation. Only after he has closed the back door behind him:*)

THERESA: He's gone.

FANT: The ideal man. That's all there is to say. Too much, really.

THERESA: I feel honored every time he comes in. He only has to pass my store and I feel honored, really. With those dark glasses! Doesn't say hello and walks straight in.

FANT: Well, it's time for me to go in. He's seen me. (*He goes into the back room.*)

THERESA: The ideal man.

WENZEL WONDRAK: (*Rushes into the store.*) Where's Millie?

(*Theresa notices him, opens her mouth and doesn't answer.*)

WONDRAK: Where's Millie?

THERESA: I dunno.

WONDRAK: (*Threatening.*) I wanna know where Millie is!

THERESA: How about showing some manners, Wenzel Wondrak.

WONDRAK: I don't have the time.

THERESA: There she comes.

MILLIE SHRIEK: (*Enters.*) Well, well, well! Wenzel Wondrak! And what, may I ask, did you bring me today?

WONDRAK: Cut the bull. I've got nothin'. Let's go outside.

THERESA: Secrets again, huh?

WONDRAK: (*In front of the store, to Millie.*) Now you put that in a safe place. I'll come get it tomorrow.

MILLIE: Where'd you get it?

WONDRAK: None of your goddam business. A raid of Barass's apartment.

MILLIE: Really!

WONDRAK: He cried like a little baby. Every week this same Mr. Joseph Barass has been bringing me half of his paycheck. For a whole year. In return, I've dropped the death penalty.

MILLIE: How on earth did he get it? He of all people, he hasn't got a penny. Where did he get it all of a sudden?

WONDRAK: Why the hell should I care? Why the hell should you? Just put it in a safe place, you hear. (*He wants to go inside.*)

MILLIE: (*Holds him back.*) Hey, can I look in it?

WONDRAK: The hell you can. I'll punch ya right in the face if you do. Wanna get caught by the old hag?

MILLIE: I'll do it in the basement.

WONDRAK: There's no light.

MILLIE: I'll bring a light.

WONDRAK: And lose it.

MILLIE: How could I ever lose *that*! I'd always find it even if the basement was twice as big. Easy. Don't worry about that.

WONDRAK: I said no and that's it. Too much junk in the basement.

MILLIE: I'll go in the attic.

WONDRAK: You might drop it. All the way down the stairs.

MILLIE: (*In the meantime she has taken the mirror out of its little case.*) But it's metal!

WONDRAK: (*Grabs both the mirror and the case.*) So it'll wear off! You'll see. It's gonna be nice 'n' shiny after a while. I'll put it back in its case. I did it before. I know exactly how it fits.

MILLIE: Jeez, you're really somethin'. Freddy ain't nothin' like that. Once he gave me (*near swooning*) his photograph.

WONDRAK: C'mon. Cut that bull, will ya. That was ten years ago and he took it back too.

MILLIE: (*Close to tears.*) Just once, please, lemme have just one little peek!

WONDRAK: If you do, we're through! Anyway, I could tell by your face, if you looked. (*He walks through the store into the back room. Millie sneaks off in tears.*)

FRITZ SHAKEE: (*Opens the door abruptly and walks toward Theresa Shriek reproaching her.*) How do you think this is going to work, Mrs. Shriek?

THERESA: (*Stammering.*) P-pardon me, Mr.—Shakee. Is something missing?

SHAKEE: The most important thing.

THERESA: Well—I could—quickly get it—if that's all right—or Millie could.

SHAKEE: I can't preside at the meeting. I need two different crates. One smaller, one bigger.

THERESA: Oh, you can have those right away Mr.—Mr. Shakee. I've got plenty of crates. (*She drags two crates over to him.*)

SHAKEE: Is there a clear difference between the two?

THERESA: Please, go ahead. See for yourself.

SHAKEE: They'll do. Do you have a black cloth?

THERESA: Sure, I've got a black cloth. (*She gets a black shawl out of a drawer.*)

(*Fred Hero appears in the door and stops respectfully.*)

SHAKEE: Let me have it. It'll do. Wondrak!

(*Wondrak enters from the back room, takes the two crates and drags them in the other room. Shakee carries the shawl. He doesn't thank Theresa. The door closes behind him.*)

THERESA: (*To anybody.*) Yessir! Like a field marshall with his dark glasses. I knew him when he still had his stutter. That was ten years ago. Next to him we certainly are an unworthy bunch. (*She notices Fred Hero. Her tone of voice changes abruptly.*) She isn't back yet. Millie, I mean.

HERO: May I kindly ask when she'll give me the pleasure to show up?

THERESA: Why don't you ask her yourself?

HERO: That's a possibility, dearest mother-in-law. However, how will this be possible when she isn't here?

THERESA: I've stopped asking her questions.

HERO: A little hanky, a little panky and everything will be all right again.

THERESA: Nothing'll be all right again.

HERO: And why, may I ask, won't anything be all right again?

THERESA: The child's lost her head.

HERO: I'd be more than happy to fit it with the finest new wig.

THERESA: That's all she needs, to make her even crazier! That girl, lemme tell you (*imploring*), that girl's vain!

HERO: She certainly's been on my back bugging me for . . . well, you know what. She wants me to break off a piece and bring it to her. How could I? I'd lose my job immediately.

MILLIE: (*Appears, she is very agitated.*) How could he? How could he! But looking at himself all day—that he can do!

HERO: I beg your pardon, if you don't mind, that's part of my job.

MILLIE: Quite a job, where they can come and lock you up any day!

HERO: Sour grapes! Sour grapes!

MILLIE: Freddy, honey, don't they have a little spare piece somewhere in that house?

HERO: Every piece is worth a fortune. Our customers are very wealthy people. You know that! We charge outrageous prices. Just think of the risk involved.

MILLIE: Why can't you take me along?

HERO: Babe, that would cost me my head.

MILLIE: Great loss it would be.

HERO: Thank you. Thank you very much. There's other fish in the pond you know. (*He goes into the back room.*)

THERESA: Boy, if he ever dares to show his face here again. What a jerk!

PREACHER CRUMB: (*Appears in the door.*) Don't lose your temper, good woman. A man is only human!

THERESA: (*Blushing.*) Lord in Heaven, Preacher Crumb in person! What an honor!

PREACHER CRUMB: Don't lose your temper, good woman. A man is only human.

THERESA: You've gotta see that jerk to believe it!

MILLIE: Mama! (*She busies herself behind the counter.*)

THERESA: First she starts a fight with him, then she's scared he won't come back. You really think you can get rid of that guy? You can insult him till you're blue in the face, you'll never get rid of him. That guy's a criminal! He comes back again and again.

CRUMB: Isn't he human like all of us? Has he not two eyes? A nose? A mouth? And has he not two honest-to-God ears?

(*Lights fade in the store.*)

THE BACK ROOM

(*Fritz Shakee sits on a big crate, in front of him a small crate, which is covered with a black cloth. Seated in front of him on three small crates lined up in a straight row are Wenzel Wondrak, François Fant and Fred Hero. All four are wearing black glasses.*)

SHAKEE: We still haven't got the situation under control. As voluntary crime fighters it is our duty to stick to our guns.

THE THREE: (*Applauding.*) Bravo!

SHAKEE: Thank you. (*Referring to the applause.*) But this isn't permitted. May I further remind you how much misery it has caused already. Is there a person alive whose heart isn't moved to bitter tears over this deplorable situation, and if there is, he certainly doesn't deserve to live another day.

FANT: Bravo! Well said! May I speak?

SHAKEE: Our next speaker is Mr. François Fant, Treasurer of the Four.

FANT: I suggest we keep a closer watch over the girls. They walk around in broad daylight and keep looking into each other's eyes. What decent man wouldn't blush at the sight of them? What can one do about the eyes? Can we discuss this matter and forward the recommended resolutions to Top of the Four.

WONDRAK: Tear out the eyes, ladies and gentlemen, tear out the eyes. It's the best method, the only cure.

SHAKEE: I am sorry but I must ask the Substitute Chairman of the Four to officially request permission to speak.

HERO: I'd like to speak now.

SHAKEE: Our next speaker is the Mediator of the Four.

HERO: Gentlemen, I for one am not for tearing out the eyes. It's no big deal to tear out eyes. If I may say so, gentlemen, anybody can do that. Instead, I suggest we approach the girls on an individual basis and tell them that they should stop looking into each other's eyes. What do they get out of it anyway! I recommend we try this first. After all, what's there to see in an eye! To put it bluntly: Nothing, gentlemen. Why don't we give it a try.

WONDRAK: Get rid of the eyes, ladies and gentlemen! I still say tear out the eyes!

SHAKEE: I must again warn the Substitute Chairman of the Four not to speak without official permission to do so. Otherwise I would be forced to impose the statutory penalty.

FANT: Too much! May I speak then.

SHAKEE: The Treasurer of the Four is next.

FANT: I have an idea. Let's have a vote. That's the smoothest solution.

SHAKEE: I agree and call for a vote. First the Substitute Chairman of the Four.

WONDRAK: Tear out the eyes, ladies and gentlemen! I still say tear out the eyes! It's the only cure, there is no other way, believe me, ladies and gentlemen, out with the eyes!

SHAKEE: The Moderator of the Four is next.

HERO: I am most definitely against it. That's no way, tearing out the eyes!

SHAKEE: One to one. May I ask the Treasurer of the Four for his position?

FANT: It's all right with me. It's something new. Can you imagine the terror? Too much!

WONDRAK: Terrific! Absolutely terrific!

SHAKEE: Last warning for the Substitute Chairman of the Four. The votes are two to one. As Chairman of the Four I shall cast my vote—in favor of tearing out the eyes. The result of the vote is three to one. The recommendation will be submitted to Top of the Four, that is to say to the Chairman at the Top of the Four. This, ladies and gentlemen, concludes today's meeting and I solemnly declare this session adjourned. You may all go home now and think some more about this issue. Our next meeting is tomorrow at 9 A.M. in my school. (*The three put their glasses away.*) Wait, one more thing, gentlemen! I am sorry, I forgot something very important. (*The three put their black glasses back on.*) I hereby suspend the adjournment of this meeting and solemnly declare it reopened.

(*Lights fade on the back room.*)

STORE

PUPPI: (*Entering.*) Good evening, Mrs. Shriek.

THERESA: How d'you do, miss. Why so late? Is anything wrong?

PUPPI: I saw your lights still on. I have a problem. I lost my flashlight and all the stores are closed now.

MILLIE: (*Nervously.*) We don't carry flashlights.

THERESA: What are you talking about? She has no idea, but still opens her big mouth. Of course I've flashlights, miss. There must be one left in stock.

MILLIE: Mama, since when do you carry flashlights?

THERESA: Since today. Isn't that too bad.

MILLIE: There's one and we need that one ourselves.

THERESA: We'll talk about that later. (*She opens the drawer.*) Here you go, miss, a flashlight, an excellent model, the last one. Wouldn't you know, looks like I have another one. No. What can this be? (*She takes a small case out of the drawer and lights it with the flashlight. She is trembling all over. Like a snake, a mirror glides out of the case in the bright beam of the flashlight. Theresa can see herself and shrieks.*) The devil! The devil! (*She holds on to the mirror and the light and doesn't move her eyes from them.*) The devil! The devil! (*She dances with the mirror and the light as if she were holding burning coals.*) The devil! The devil! (*Millie and the Preacher rush toward her. With big, terrified eyes, Puppi shrinks back toward the door staring at the possessed woman.*)

MILLIE: Mama, for God's sake, be quiet.

CRUMB: (*Wrests the flashlight from her hands and casually puts it in his pocket.*) Good woman, what's the matter with you? Calm down. Please. What's wrong? The devil, sister, would never enter this clean store.

(*As soon as the flashlight has been taken from her, Theresa faints. The Preacher holds her in his arms. Millie holds her mouth shut. Puppi disappears quietly.*)

MILLIE: She must still be holding something. She won't open her hand.

CRUMB: Now open your hand, sister, go on, open your hand.

THERESA: (*With choked voice.*) I won't give it to her. Not to her. She's possessed.

CRUMB: Give it to me, sister, just give it to me. Relax, I only want to help you. There! (*Theresa opens her hand. He sees the mirror and recoils. But he doesn't let go of her hand.*) I'll take it. I'll do it for you. You're a good woman. If they find that on you, they'll kill you. I'll destroy it. (*With a very rigid motion he takes the mirror and puts it in the same pocket as the flashlight.*)

(*Millie lets go of her mother and sobs heartbreakingly.*)

THERESA: (*Whimpering softly.*) The devil! The devil!

STREET AT NIGHT

(*Preacher Crumb walks down the street. It is very dark, his right trouser pocket is lit. That's where he carries the mirror and the flashlight which he forgot to turn off in the rush. Sometimes he leans toward the opposite side as if to balance the weight on the right side. His hand frequently moves toward the pocket, but each time it withdraws very quickly: "Hot. Hot. Good God is that hot." His pocket outlines the street. It is dimly lit. The few lanterns are so high up that their light doesn't seem much stronger than the one in his pocket. The dark silence all around is suddenly pierced by a groan. Crumb stops. Not far from him, but very low, probably on the floor, there is a light similar to his. He approaches it hesitatingly. The groaning gets stronger. A few more steps, more steadily now, and he reaches the light.*)

CRUMB: What's the matter? Are you hurt? (*Groaning.*) I want to help you. What's the matter? (*Groaning.*) Poor man! In such pain! Let me help you, poor soul. (*Groaning with the word "light" coming through.*) You want light? Just a minute, good man, just a minute! (*He kneels down, pulls a flashlight from the pocket of the man on the floor and looks at him in the light.*) He isn't bleeding. I see no blood. (*Groaning.*) You must be wounded very badly. Internally, I guess. Let me help you, good man.

(*Groaning: "Light! Light!" Crumb quickly puts away the flashlight of the man on the floor. He puts it in his own left pocket and lifts him with great effort. Then he helps him, or rather carries him, to the nearest lamppost and props him gently against it. He pulls out the man's flashlight and examines his face, more thoroughly this time. But the man sways.*)

CRUMB: So, now, let me have a closer look at you, brother. I'll be very careful, don't you worry. I won't hurt you. Come, come. Relax. It's not that bad. You don't even look sick! A young man like you! And strong as can be! So full of life! How old can you possibly be? Thirty, maximum. Look at those rosy cheeks! A face like an apple. You'll live through it, believe me, brother. One can live through everything. What did they do to you? Now, be a good boy and open your mouth! Look at those gorgeous teeth! A blessing, what a blessing! Now I could pray as much as I want for such a set of teeth, it wouldn't do any good, 'cause with me it's too late. But you! Some teeth! One pearlier than the next and not one missin'. What a sight! What a blessing! So full of life! Now where does it hurt, tell me? Where? (*The man has stopped groaning. He is silent.*) Of course, you've trouble talking. Why don't you stay right here. I'll get help. I'll be right back.

THE MAN: (*Dryly.*) My flashlight!

CRUMB: Oh, you want your flashlight. Here you go.

THE MAN: (*Turns on the light, says "Thank you" and walks off a completely healthy man.*)

CRUMB: (*Staring after him.*) What was this all about? He wasn't hurt at all. Poor deceitful sinner! (*As he says "sinner" he quickly checks his pocket. Then he walks on, much more slowly than before, as if he was still hoping for the man to come back with his light and with his groaning. But instead of just one light, many lights appear, the street is filling up with lights and groans. The more there are, the better one can hear their words. The threats are outdoing one another.*)

Help! I'm suffocating!
I'm dying of thirst! Water! Water!
I'm dying!
I'm bleeding to death!
Ooooohhhhh!

CRUMB: What do you want? What do you want? I'm all by myself. I can't help you. (*Suddenly something jumps up next to him, screaming "What's that in your pocket?" Crumb recoils. He walks faster. He sighs. After a while he says loudly:*) Oh my God, is it really that bad not to be able to see oneself? (*At that moment a man appears in front of him.*)

BLEISS: You want to see yourself?

CRUMB: Wh-what?

BLEISS: Do you want to see yourself?

CRUMB: Are you . . . kidding me?

BLEISS: It doesn't cost much. You won't regret it.

CRUMB: Good man . . .

BLEISS: Don't give me that! You can afford it!

CRUMB: But I . . .

BLEISS: Ten shillings for two minutes. I'll provide the light. (*A small flashlight lights up. We recognize S. Bleiss.*)

CRUMB: Oh brother.

BLEISS: Here, get under the awning. Don't be afraid.

CRUMB: Are you sure you know what you are doing?

BLEISS: That's my problem. Do you want to see yourself?

CRUMB: Look around you! Have you no heart? Look at all those lights!

BLEISS: They're scum. They have no money. What do you know. These people haven't seem themselves in years. They're just waiting for a few nice words. The lowest trash!

CRUMB: Aren't you scared, brother?

BLEISS: Now I get it. You're in the racket too. Why are you wasting my time then? You're crazy. You have it in your trouser pocket! Your flashlight's lit. Your pocket gives you away. Let me tell you, you're crazy!

(He disappears. Crumb starts running. Someone is coming his way. He jumps out of the way. He falls and groans. When he gets up his flashlight is still burning. He puts both hands around it and tries, with great difficulty, to walk this way. Someone else is coming toward him. He seeks cover under a huge bay window which is brightly lit. He holds his hands over his own light, which seems much weaker here. This way he almost fades into the darkness. In the drawing room above, a man is pacing up and down. The windows are wide open. The person whom Crumb tried to avoid now enters the house and soon becomes visible in the drawing room. It is a lady.)

LEDA FRESH BREEZE: That's just awful. I can't take it anymore. Henry, it can't go on like this!

HENRY BREEZE: What's the matter now, Leda dear?

LEDA: I am scared! All those people lying on the ground, groaning. It's awful. It's so senseless, everything!

HENRY: Calm down, it's not that bad.

LEDA: It's easy for you to say. You don't know. I do. Every night the same. All day long I tremble at the thought of going home. That's how scared I am. Every time I step on one, I want to scream!

HENRY: Then watch your step!

LEDA: But there are so many! And most of them aren't lit at all. They just lie down in the middle of the street and you can't get through. And if you happen to notice one in time, you have to go out of your way to be nice to him before he'll move out of your way. But God forbid you don't notice and you step on one! Then all hell breaks loose! The guy'll scream as if you're trying to kill him. You've got to pick him up and check him, you have to comfort and flatter him. These people are literally dying for you to say something about them. They don't know themselves. No one who's able to talk will talk to them. That's why they throw themselves on the street at night waiting for someone to fall over them. That's their way of getting attention. It's blackmail, really. These people are so starved, it's unbelievable! I am so scared! One day one of these guys'll just hit me over the head and that'll be it.

HENRY: No one is going to do that, Leda dear. No one's that stupid. If he'd shut you up for good, you'd be of no more use to him: quite the contrary, he'll always make sure to be exceptionally nice to you.

LEDA: You don't know those people. They are not that reasonable. I can't help myself, they scare me to death!

HENRY: A doctor like you should have better nerves, my dear.

LEDA: You've got the wrong idea about my patients, Henry. You won't find that kind in our sanitarium. Thank God, we don't have those. I know a great deal, I may know a lot of things but I do not know how to handle a case like this!

HENRY: How could you? They can't be treated individually. They must be dealt with as a whole. That's what politics are for.

LEDA: Listen, Henry. I don't mind working for both of us. I've never reproached you for not earning any money. I know, you're something special. You're preparing for something really great. I know it. But I can't take this neighborhood anymore. We're the only civilized people living here. Believe me, the rest is trash. You are such a dreamer, you don't notice. I know. Henry, I implore you, let's move out of this neighborhood!

HENRY: I am very sorry, Leda dear. But I can only tell you what I've already told you yesterday, and the day before yesterday, and the day before. It is impossible. Finis.

LEDA: You don't love me.

HENRY: I do love you. But I also need this atmosphere. Granted, these people don't really know who I am. But they feel it. I am their sun. Their source of light. I radiate. I work on myself every day. And I have found myself. At night I keep my windows open and I can sense how they listen to every word I say. Leda dear, isn't this a wonderful life? And when I have enough, I close the windows and pull the curtains.

(*The scum has gathered in front of the window. People in rags tiptoe to the alcove. The light from the talkative salon shines on many heads who listen in ecstasy.*)

LEDA: Yes, that's wonderful, but I . . .

HENRY: I'm sorry, Leda, but there's nothing I can do about it. It's a law of nature. But I have a present for you.

LEDA: For me? You know there's only one present I want and that's the one I won't get.

HENRY: I have thought about it, Leda dear. Today everybody has his own song, which belongs only to him, and no one can take it away from him. I can understand that. At least, you need to hear yourself in a very special way, if you can't see yourself.

LEDA: Yes. Yes.

HENRY: You shall have your song, Leda. I had to say no to you all this time because it would have interfered too much with my life. But now I've become so sure of myself that nothing can throw me off my path—except for a source of energy more powerful than myself—and that has yet to be found.

LEDA: What? I can have my song? My very own song? Just for me? And I may sing it too?

HENRY: Yes, my dear, I think about you a lot, you just don't feel it.

LEDA: Thank you, Henry. You do love me after all!

HENRY: You see, I love you. But in return, I'm asking you a small favor. I would like to ask you not to call me by my first name anymore. It interferes with my development. And I am not the type of man who doesn't care. I cringe every time you call me Henry. And it always costs me a lot of time and nerves to recover. Often it throws me back for weeks, if not months. That doesn't make any sense, does it? Actually, I find it quite presumptuous to use first names, at least with exceptional people. But that doesn't mean that you have to call me "sir." There are many ways to get around it. Right?

(*He walks to the window and closes it. He also closes the curtains, and now the window looks like an empty screen. The heads outside turn away. The light goes out. The people disappear. Everywhere we can hear the groaning on the ground again. Crumb sneaks away, bent over, as if crawling. He too is groaning now.*)

MARIE'S KITCHEN

(*Located stage right. The room, spotless, sparkling and orderly, is all Marie's doing. She is putting dishes into a cabinet. Near the window, not far from her, Preacher Crumb. For the time being, stage left remains dark.*)

CRUMB: So it goes. So it goes. You are alive and well. And suddenly you're dead.

MARIE: Not me. Don't look at me.

CRUMB: Who knows? Who knows? Maybe in less than five minutes.

MARIE: Not me. I tell you.

CRUMB: I pray to the Lord that you're right, my child. But don't be too sure. Our Lord and Master doesn't like that.

MARIE: I already have a master. I don't need two.

CRUMB: Why must you be so mean, my child? No one's hurting you! Aren't you alive? Don't you enjoy the warmth of the sun?

MARIE: The sun? Big deal. Everybody can have sun.

CRUMB: What more do you need for your happiness? I am talking about a nice girl who does her work and does it well. She has a roof over her head and plenty of food on the table. Her work used to be much tougher in the old days. They still had windows then, made of ugly, transparent glass which had to be cleaned. Now the glass is gray like concrete and it needs very little cleaning.

MARIE: Clean windows? Was fun! Gentlemen used to look up from street. All gentlemen, who walked by, stopped and looked up, looked at me. And now? No more windows. Finished.

CRUMB: Years ago there lived in this town a sweet, virtuous girl. One day as she was cleaning windows, she fell down and died.

MARIE: So, she beat us all to heaven.

CRUMB: If she hasn't been looking in the mirror too much! I've never been in her room. I can't say how it looked there, in the most hidden corners of her little room. Secretly, she might have been the biggest sinner.

MARIE: I've nothing in my room. Nothing I want to have!

CRUMB: But it could be a different story, couldn't it, Marie? A decent man will marry you.

MARIE: Don't need man. Don't need it.

CRUMB: Do you really know what you are saying? A human being, all alone, gets terribly lost in the dark of the night. A human being, all alone, is vain. You too, dear Marie. What if a decent man comes along to reach for this hard-working hand? Marie will take care of his home. And he will bring home the daily bread. And they shall live together in peace and modesty. Perhaps this man isn't so far away, Marie.

MARIE: I know. I know. I don't need man. What for? So I fight all day?

CRUMB: Dear Marie, will you ever listen again to the true calling of your heart?

MARIE: Not with the people I work for. Never! In old days they got along fine. Now they fight all day long. Always about singing. No one lets other sing. Everybody wants to sing. And you should hear them talk. They always talk. And when they stop talking, they start all over again. Right away they start fight. They call me. If I don't come, they hit each other, with fists. I don't need man. I need something else! It's something else I need.

CRUMB: Dear child, what you need is a sin.

MARIE: Yes? Was it sin in old days? No!

CRUMB: It always was a sin. Only people didn't know. Now they know.

MARIE: How can you know, all of a sudden. I don't get it!

CRUMB: Believe me, child, it always was a big sin. In fact, it is the biggest sin. If you indulge in it, your fate will be terrible indeed. Our Lord isn't kidding.

MARIE: Since when?

CRUMB: Always! Always! But in the old days people were blinded. Trust me, Marie!

MARIE: Go away, stupid man. Always same old story, every day. I don't need man! I need something else! I need mirror, which was in my room. They took it. I need mirror. Now I am mess. Ten years I am mess! I need my mirror. You end in garbage, let me tell you, with messy woman! I am mess now! I need my mirror! In garbage, you hear, that's where you end, with messy woman. I need something else, yes: Mirror! Mirror! Mirror!

CRUMB: (*Very solemnly.*) You shall have your wish, dear child. I have brought you your medicine. A very dangerous medicine. This medicine will cure you of all your sinful wishes. Here is a mirror. Take it! And if by tomorrow it doesn't burn your hands hotter than hell fire, I give up on your soul, Marie. (*He leaves the kitchen.*)

MARIE: Finally! (*She gets busy with the mirror.*)

THE KALDAUNS' DINING ROOM

(*Light stage left. Someone is leaving through the dark corridor, which connects the kitchen and the dining room.*)

LYA KALDAUN: (*Standing alone at the table.*) A dreadful person. Ought to be scrubbing toilets. But no, that kind of person wants to be personal maid to a lady.

(*Knocking at the door.*)

LYA: Come in!

MILLIE SHRIEK: (*Enters.*) Ma'am, may I?

LYA: You are the fifth applicant today. Unbelievable . . . the types that show up. Are you going to disappoint me too?

MILLIE: Time will tell, ma'am.

LYA: Time! Very good. What's your name?

MILLIE: Millie, if you please.

LYA: You call that a name? Millie! It makes me sick. Every other servant's called Millie nowadays. I need a personal maid.

MILLIE: Yes, ma'am!

LYA: Millie. How do you get such a name?

MILLIE: A good fairy put it in my crib.

LYA: I would've liked to see that good fairy. She probably was a washerwoman . . . in woolen underwear.

MILLIE: That's what I think too, ma'am.

LYA: A good fairy! What's it like, you think?

MILLIE: Like you, ma'am, if you please.

LYA: Like me?

MILLIE: Just like you, ma'am. A beautiful lady is like the sun, it shines for everyone.

LYA: Everyone? What makes you say that?

MILLIE: That's how they say.

LYA: Tell me, why am I like a good fairy?

MILLIE: Ma'am has eyes like stars, a rose of a mouth . . .

LYA: And the hair?

MILLIE: Hair as black as an Arabian night.

LYA: Tell me, what would a man think of me?

MILLIE: The male species is forever indebted to you.

LYA: But let's say, a very special man. Let's say a chairman of the board.

MILLIE: Everybody considers it a great honor to be running after you.

LYA: Even a chairman of the board?

MILLIE: Yes, ma'am.

LYA: Have you been employed before?

MILLIE: This is the first time, if you please.

LYA: You see, I'd like to train someone. Just for me. How old are you?

MILLIE: I'm young, ma'am. But by far not as young as you, ma'am.

LYA: How old would you guess I am?

MILLIE: Twenty-three maximum. Maybe 21. Maybe 22. But it couldn't be 23. I was wrong, please excuse my error.

LYA: What do you mean? Are you serious?

MILLIE: Yes, ma'am!

LYA: So you've never been employed before. Do you have problems at home? I mean, because you want to leave. You aren't pregnant, I hope!

MILLIE: Oh no, ma'am, absolutely not.

LYA: Then why?

MILLIE: To put it simply: I don't get along.

LYA: That's what I thought. Are you spoiled?

MILLIE: No, ma'am, if you please.

LYA: I find you quite acceptable. You're the first one. Except for the name.

MILLIE: May I tell you a riddle, beautiful lady?

LYA: I beg your pardon?

MILLIE: Just what my new name should be.

LYA: What do you suggest?

MILLIE: The prize-winning answer is: Leonia.

LYA: Leonia. I don't get it.

MILLIE: You're right. It's too much. I beg your pardon.

LYA: Any other suggestions?

MILLIE: Mary, if you please.

LYA: Now you're talking. Very good. Do you talk back?

MILLIE: Time will tell, madam.

LYA: Mary, you will be my personal maid. But that means you've got to move fast. We'll soon let go of Marie, our cook. She's getting too old. She's been with us for thirteen years. I think we've done enough for her. My husband is speechless. It can't go on forever. We won't have it. When we let go of Marie, you will also take over the kitchen. That won't be too much since there are no windows to clean. Can you believe how hard it used to be for a maid!

MILLIE: Beautiful lady, may I kindly ask you a favor?

LYA: What else do you want?

MILLIE: There's a song: "I'm kissing your hand, madam!"

LYA: I understand.

(*Millie grabs Lya's hand and kisses it.*)

(*Marie is busy with her mirror. After a first long look she shakes her head. She gets a cloth, picks up the tiny mirror and cleans it thoroughly as if it were a big, heavy object. The second look increases her discontent. She starts to polish again, more vehemently than before, her nervous movements indicating anger. At the moment when Millie Shriek kisses Madam's hand, Marie stamps her foot angrily: "Is fake! Is fake!" Millie Shriek exits through the corridor. Lights fade stage left. Marie gives the mirror another try. There's a knock at the kitchen door. She quickly puts the mirror away and calls out:*)

MARIE: Who is it?

FRANCES NADA: (*Enters.*) Have you got something to eat for me, Miss Marie?

MARIE: Ah, Frances Nada. Yes, I have something.

FRANCES: Now I've got it in my knees too. Arthritis! And my back! I can feel it when I walk. I always think now I'm gonna fall. Old age, Miss Marie, it's a problem.

MARIE: Oh, stop it.

FRANCES: I could use new teeth. Look here, Miss Marie. Not a tooth in my mouth. You see! But it ain't for me, I want you to know. It's only for Frankie, if I find him again. He'd never recognize me without my teeth.

MARIE: Oh stop it, will you! Here's something to eat.

FRANCES: Listen to me. It's forty years now that I've lost him. He might not recognize me anymore. 'Cause I've become very old, Miss Marie. Not a tooth in my mouth. You saw it. Now there're some who'd be very bitter about all this. Not me. I ain't bitter. 'Cause there ain't no need for him to recognize me. I'd recognize him anyways.

MARIE: Stop it and eat. Stupid woman. Always same old stories. Every day! Five years she sat in jail for her brother and now she starts again on him.

FRANCES: Oh yes, five years I sat—for him. They took 'im away. At the fire. Remember the big fire? I was lookin' for him, 'cause a porter's got lots of work at that kind o' fire. So I look and I look. Now, listen to me, Miss Marie, I just can feel that he's there. You know. I've got this special sense for my Frankie, but only for him. You don't believe me, do you, Miss Marie. Now listen to me carefully: I come to the fire. And just as I get to the fire, I find him. That was ten years ago. At that time it's been exactly thirty years. So I find him and just as I find him, there comes a gentleman, a fine gentleman, an' he takes him away from me. He takes him away from me. "Thief," I yell, "Let 'im go! Thieves! Don't hurt 'im! Let 'im go!" "All right," the gentlemen said, "If you can't shut up, we'll lock you up! That'll get you five years in jail." "Fine," says I, "but my brother, I won't let you have my brother, not my brother, not my brother! No!"

MARIE: Stop screaming, Frances, eat now! When master comes, he'll throw you out.

FRANCES: Now I've lost my appetite. People keep asking me: Can't you forget

him, Frances Nada? And I says: No! Never. I can never forget him! You
see, Miss Marie, he does everything I tell 'im. Those folks he works
for—he ain't chargin' them enough. The kind o' porter he is, the stuff he
can carry, you wouldn't believe it. Frankie, I say to him, you've gotta
charge more. Don't be a fool. They'll laugh about you, those rich folk. So
what does he do? Listen to this, Miss Marie. Right away he starts charging
what he deserves. See, he knows me. He knows I mean well.

MARIE: You know that one, Frances Nada? (*Sings.*) At night, at night, when
love shines bright . . .

FRANCES: Go on, how does it go?

MARIE: I don't know. I haven't learned it yet. At night, at night, when love
shines bright.

FRANCES: Who's singing it in this house?

MARIE: Only me. It's my song. No one else sings it. You think I sing other
people's songs? Stupid woman! You stop it now with your stupid brother
all the time!

FRANCES: I've got a song too, Miss Marie. You know that one? You, you,
yes, only you! I've worked it out all by myself. (*She sings, with more and more
excitement in her old, brittle voice.*) You, you, yes, only you. You know that's
for my Frankie. You, you, yes only you!

MARIE: Is pretty. Never heard it. Can't remember all the songs there are.

FRANCES: You know, Miss Marie, I ain't gonna beg forever. I'm gonna get
rich someday!

MARIE: Stop it, will you! You—rich?

FRANCES: It'll have to happen, Miss Marie. I've gotta save up for Frankie.
What's he gonna do in his old age? You know how old he is, Miss Marie?
Now listen to me, Miss Marie: He is old—past eighty. And still so strong
you wouldn't believe it! But that's gonna be over too some day, that
strength of his. It ain't lastin' forever, that's for sure. Then what? What's
he gonna do without a single penny to his name? Now, you see, Miss
Marie, that's why I save up for him. He's got only me, nobody else. Nobody! You know, what I'd need, Miss Marie (*very secretively*), a shard!

MARIE: A shard? You? Oh, stop it! What will you do with shard?

FRANCES: I'd go door to door! I'd make money! You can make a fortune with
it! I mean, just a little shard, a mirror, as they say. For five years I've been
lookin' for a shard, I just can't find one.

MARIE: (*Pulls her little mirror out of her blouse.*) There, Frances Nada, there's mirror for you.

FRANCES: Lord Almighty, Miss Marie, you! My dear, sweet Miss Marie's got
a shard! Where on earth did you get that shard? And that shard's now really mine? For God's sake, dear Miss Marie, I can't accept that shard, really!
But where on earth did you get that shard?

MARIE: (*Furiously.*) Is fake, dreck. That's mirror? That dreck? I don't need
dreck. I don't need fake. You think I look like that? Never! (*She points at the*

mirror, without looking in it again, while Frances has already grabbed it.) At night, at night, when love shines bright!

KALDAUN: (*Who comes home for lunch, outside, in the corridor.*) Baby, you dance just like my wife.

FRANCES: (*Is courteous enough to watch Marie's outburst with great amazement for a while, finally give in to her own great joy. Mirror in hand, she dances and screams around the kitchen.*) You, you, yes only you!

MARIE: (*Still furious.*) At night, at night, when love shines bright!

EUGENE: (*Opens the kitchen door, faster and more forcefully than is to be expected from him.*) Marie, I've told you a thousand times: you shouldn't sing! Simple as that!

FRANCES: (*Quickly hides her shard.*) Oh my God, it's you sir, such a kind, dear, noble master!

EUGENE: What's a beggarwoman doing in my kitchen?

FRANCES: (*Tippytoeing toward him.*) You, you, yes only you.

EUGENE: That's just what we needed! Begging isn't enough, I see. Now she has to sing too. So she sings, she has the chutzpah to sing, just like that. You, you, yes only you! Begging's one thing. But singing, singing! I live here too! And I won't have it. If Lya could've seen that! Today you're fired for the last time! You, you, yes only you! How dare you sing, you impertinent old hag! How old are you anyway? Knows no shame. Simple as that. You just let me catch you singing one more time—I'll have you arrested! You, you, yes only you! I'll show you, you you, yes only you! (*He starts hitting old Frances.*) Everybody's singing nowadays! Everybody! Everybody sings. Lya sings. The children sing. Marie sings. The beggarwoman! Everybody sings. Just like that. I live here too. And I won't have it. First of all, wash your filthy mouth, old hag! Simple as that. Then sing. You, you, yes only you. I could kill her! And you, Marie, you're going. You leave this house for the last time today!

MARIE: You watch me leave! I get married, I want you to know, me, married!

EUGENE: (*Wipes his hands, exits, slamming the door and shouting.*) Baby, you dance just like my wife!

THE STREET

(*Barass collides with Killoff. They resemble each other. However, Barass looks poor and raggedy, while Killoff is elegant and groomed.*)

KILLOFF: Would you please watch where you're going! I mean, really!

BARASS: Oh, take it easy.

KILLOFF: How d'you like that. Bumps right into me.

BARASS: I'm sorry, sir. Nothin' happened anyways.

KILLOFF: Look here, you've put wrinkles in my coat. It's just what I've been waiting for.

BARASS: If that's your only problem . . .

KILLOFF: Now that really is too much. Who do you think you are? (*Only now he looks at the loudmouth and recoils at the sight of him.*) Say, how on earth did you get here?

BARASS: On my two legs. Say, you do look familiar.

KILLOFF: You do too. I mean, really. But the way you look. I mean, aren't you embarrassed? That suit of yours! (*He feels Barass's suit.*)

BARASS: (*Feels Killoff's suit.*) Permit me. I dunno what I'm doin', actually. Expensive stuff!

KILLOFF: Well, I'll be darn! Say "Ah."

BARASS: Ah!

KILLOFF: There you go. Same teeth. Strange. Could you lean your head a bit—I mean, over to me?

BARASS: Sure, why not? (*They move their heads closer to each other and begin to touch each other. Barass, who has no hat, takes Killoff's hat.*)

KILLOFF: Identical. (*Barass puts on the hat.*) Especially with the hat.

BARASS: Wait till you see me in that coat! Watch. (*Takes off Killoff's coat as if from a small child, then puts it on himself.*) Well?

KILLOFF: Fabulous! I mean. The greatest pleasure in years.

BARASS: Jeez, if I'd only known earlier.

KILLOFF: In the same town. So close to each other. What a pleasure!

BARASS: In times like these.

KILLOFF: That we didn't meet before!

BARASS: A true miracle!

KILLOFF: Joseph, of course?

BARASS: What else?

KILLOFF: One shouldn't get married. The one time I'm going out without my wife, something great is happening to me. I mean, really. She's busy right now fixing my bath, so I went out all by myself.

BARASS: That's what I say: Broads! They did me in all right—you wouldn't believe it.

KILLOFF: Sure. Of course. That's understood. Same here.

BARASS: One oughta stay a bachelor! That brings luck.

KILLOFF: I'm going to throw mine out. First chance I get.

BARASS: Me too. That's the way: throw 'em out!

KILLOFF: We could meet more often. How's your health?

BARASS: A-OK. Nothing's wrong with my health. Look! (*He shows his muscles; Killoff shows his.*) Oh well . . .

KILLOFF: (*Looks at Barass's shoes.*) Those shoes . . . that's a bit much.

BARASS: You better not look. It ain't worth it.

KILLOFF: I must tell you honestly, my friend. Those shoes . . . I mean, really!

BARASS: Well, lemme tell ya! I've gotta give away half of my paycheck. There's this dirty bastard blackmailin' me. He gets half my paycheck. I could kill that pig!

KILLOFF: How's that? How come? Paycheck?

BARASS: Yeah, my paycheck. I'm a packer.

KILLOFF: Really! Very peculiar, I mean . . . Well, why don't you give me back my hat, sir! My head's cold and I don't want to get sick. Especially not before my bath. I also need my coat back.

BARASS: Say what? You gave these things to me! That hat was a gift and that coat was a gift too. And those shoes . . . I didn't even want 'em.

KILLOFF: Now stop making such a fuss! I don't have time.

BARASS: You've gotta be outta your goddam mind! You think I'm your puppet, which you dress 'n' undress as you please?

KILLOFF: I was wrong about you. That hurts. It really hurts. I don't know if I'll ever get over it. But hurry now and give me my coat and hat!

BARASS: You're wastin' your time, mister!

KILLOFF: I'm warning you! I am well known in this town. I'll have you arrested. You stole those things. Even a child can see that.

EMILY FANT: (*Comes rushing down the street.*) My child! I'm looking for my child. Where's my child? That's no way to work! My child! Have you seen my child? Oh, hello, monsieur!

KILLOFF: That's a surprise, isn't it. I can't even raise my hat today. That man is wearing it. I mean, really . . .

MME. FANT: Now don't become unfaithful to me!

KILLOFF: Believe me, I've got other things to worry about! How's business?

MME. FANT: Busy, busy, busy! François has left me again. That child! He won't do anything for me! Nothing but work. Day and night. Night and day! If I dare say anything to him, he's insulted. You'd think he owes me some consideration!

KILLOFF: You certainly can't trust a stranger. They'll cheat you left and right.

MME. FANT: That's exactly what I keep telling him. I'm lucky when I finally get him to the cash register. How can I have a stranger handle my money? They'll cheat you left and right. Now I've got to go look for him. Meanwhile I have to pay someone to sit behind the cash register.

KILLOFF: I know what you mean, madame. I too just had a horrible experience.

BARASS: (*Throws him the coat and the hat.*) Here! You can stick 'em you know where. I'm fine the way I am. You really think I need your crap. (*Exits.*)

MME. FANT: I know him. Economy class, of course. A frequent guest. A simple laborer, a good customer. And so dependable! As soon as he gets his paycheck, he brings it straight to us.

KILLOFF: Let me give you some advice. You better watch out with that man! His face is misleading. At first I trusted him too. But just take a look at that man's clothes. Inexcusable!

MME. FANT: You're absolutely right, my friend. You're always right. From now on he won't be admitted to my sanitarium. As you wish.

KILLOFF: You're an intelligent woman. But you wouldn't believe what just happened to me! Just now! Just awful. I'm afraid I won't get over it.

MME. FANT: Come, see us, monsieur. We have class, we've pizzazz, you'll always find exactly what you want. With us, the customer is king! Without you our luxury cabins seem so lonely.

KILLOFF: Well, maybe I'll drop in later. Because right now I'm furious. And I also have to take my bath today. I'm afraid I caught a cold. Don't you have the feeling that man's a photographer?

MME. FANT: Right! I've always had that feeling. The way he resembles you. That man's got to be stopped right away.

KILLOFF: You said it! I've already stopped a photographer once, a woman. She got five years in jail. But this one seems much more dangerous. A blackmailer!

MME. FANT: You're probably right, monsieur. You're right. I hope you'll soon give us the pleasure. You didn't happen to see my François?

KILLOFF: I've got other worries, dear lady. Kindly see for yourself where you can find the brat. I really don't know how I'm going to survive this. I'm afraid I won't.

MME. FANT: (*From far away.*) My child! Where's my child? Have you seen my child? My child!

A VERY SMALL STUDIO APARTMENT

(*Austerely furnished. The bed, which takes up most of the room, looks as if it had never been used. Fritz Shakee sits stiffly in a straight back chair staring straight ahead. He doesn't move. Heidi, his bride, stands behind his chair, her body and face expressing fear and despair.*)

HEIDI: Come on now. What's the matter, huh? (*Shakee remains silent.*) What's wrong with my sweety? (*Shakee remains silent.*) What're you so upset about? Why won't my sweety talk to me? (*Shakee remains silent.*) I haven't done anything to you! I didn't call you Fritzl. Or Fritz. Just sweety! You didn't mind me calling you that! What're you so upset about? Friedrich! (*Shakee quivers ever so slightly.*) Friedrich! Can't you hear me? Friedrich! (*Shakee quivers.*) Friedrich! Friedrich! (*Shakee quivers.*) Now you can't even tell me why you're not talking? (*Shakee remains silent.*) Friedrich! You've got to get to school. You're late. Don't you hear! The school! (*Shakee remains silent.*) You can't just stay home! If you aren't sick, you can't just stay home from work! (*Shakee remains silent.*) Do you hear me, Friedrich? I can't always just talk to myself! Four days now you've been putting me through this! If only I'd know what's wrong with you. Don't you understand? (*Crying softly.*) I'm so worried, I could die!

(*Shakee remains silent.*)

HEIDI: (*Abruptly.*) Friedrich! Friedrich! For God's sake, the meeting! You've got to go to the meeting! They came today to tell you that the meeting'll be earlier. I completely forgot, 'cause I'm so worried! The meeting's at eleven. The meeting! Friedrich! The meeting! (*Shakee quivers again at the mention of his name.*) Friedrich, they can't go on without you. You're very special. They said that if you don't show up, the meeting's for the birds. The meeting, Friedrich! The meeting's for the birds if you don't show up! They need you there. Without you they're lost! (*She sobs. Shakee stops quivering as soon as she starts sobbing.*) D'you want the doctor? I'll go get the doctor. I'm so worried, I could die!

FRANCES NADA: (*Enters. She carries a huge box of matches.*) D'you need anything, miss? Is there anything you need?

HEIDI: (*Crying.*) I'd need the doctor. But I don't dare. If I go get the doctor, it's all over between us. That's what he keeps tellin' me. But I can't always talk just to myself. He hasn't said a word in four days.

FRANCES: Just wait, wait, miss. I'll see what I can do. Let me see.

(*She scampers around Shakee, adjusting him in the chair. She squeezes his head and shoulders, lifts up his chin, hits him over the nose with one finger and punches his chest with her old, tiny fist. He remains rigid as before.*)

FRANCES: There's nothing you can do, miss. Not even the doctor'll do him any good. No doctor can help this man. Nothin'll help. Do you know what he's got? Now you listen to me, miss! He's got the mirror sickness.

(*Up to this point Heidi has been holding her breath. At the word "mirror" she breaks into tears.*)

FRANCES: You'll have to get a mirror for him. Otherwise he'll never get well and you might have to have him put away. 'Cause without a mirror, he'll never get well again and then he won't do you any good. I know. I've seen it happen. Lots o' times. You need a mirror, miss, that's all there is to it. It's the only cure.

HEIDI: (*Sobbing.*) How am I gonna get one? Where am I supposed to get a . . . a . . . m-mirror? I don't have one.

FRANCES: There're ways to get a mirror. It just costs a lot o' money.

HEIDI: I don't have any. Fritzl never has any money. It all goes into his meetings. That's why you'd never find a penny in this house.

FRANCES: Oh you poor thing. Can't even spare ten shillings. What a shame. That's all it would cost to get him cured. Ten shillings.

HEIDI: Nothin'. I've got nothin'. That's the way he is. That's my Fritzl.

FRANCES: Oh well. Now if you won't tell on me, I've got one, right here. But don't you tell on me! I'll do it for you. It won't cost you anything, 'cause you're such a poor little thing.

(Heidi starts laughing and crying at the same time. Frances gets busy. She produces the tiny round shard. Hiding it carefully in her hand, she approaches Shakee from the back and climbs on a footstool. Then, not without great effort, she suddenly reaches over his shoulder and holds the mirror up to his face.)

FRANCES: Now you call 'im, miss!

HEIDI: *(Louder each time.)* Friedrich! Friedrich! Friedrich!

(Shakee comes to life. He sees himself. He wakes up. A solid rock transforms into a spindly tree.)

HEIDI: Friedrich! You've got to get to the meeting! Friedrich!

(Frances remains motionless, with the mirror in her hand.)

SHAKEE: *(As if in a dream.)* I've got to get to the meeting. I don't have time.

FRANCES: He's back to normal. *(She jumps down from the footstool.)* Now don't get me in trouble, miss! For you it's free. Good-bye. Don't tell! *(Swiftly she hobbles out of the study. Heidi says nothing.)*

SHAKEE: *(Jumping up suddenly.)* Who was here just now?

HEIDI: No one. You had a dream.

SHAKEE: A mirror was here. Who was it?

HEIDI: Oh, stop it. No one was here.

SHAKEE: How often did I tell you that you must never lie to me? *(Heidi remains silent.)* You admit that you were lying? *(Heidi remains silent.)* What's the punishment you deserve? *(Heidi remains silent.)* What punishment have I decided on, once and for all, for lying?

HEIDI: Do with me whatever you want. But don't you hurt that poor little granny. She's cured you. Mirror-sick, that's what you were. Very sick! I don't know what I would've done if she wouldn't have come by.

SHAKEE: What did she look like?

HEIDI: I can't tell you. I promised her I wouldn't tell on her.

SHAKEE: That's right. You have to keep your promise. But I didn't promise anything. I have ways to find her.

HEIDI: What if they find out that she cured you?

SHAKEE: I am Chairman of the Four. I have ways to find her. "Poor little granny," you said. That'll do.

THE STREET

(Frankie Nada, stage left, in his old spot. Stage right, very scared and ready to take off: Frances Nada. François Fant, humming and singing, comes strolling down the center street: "I'm kissing your hand, madame.")

FANT: That hairdresser's got nerves! Stealing my song! (*He stops in front of a window, sings his song, but no one appears. He says "Fabulous," and walks on. Reaching the main street he first looks right, then left. As soon as he notices both Nadas, he starts to laugh loudly. It is a tough, sober laugh. Then he turns to Frankie.*) Dear friend, have you heard the latest?

NADA: Oh my God, it's you sir. I haven't seen you in such a long time. Don't you look gorgeous!

FANT: No deal today, my friend. But I want to ask you something. Have you heard the latest? Have I got something for you today!

NADA: What could it be, sir, gorgeous sir, what is it?

FANT: Now we've got the death penalty. For flattery that is. Anyone caught in the act . . . well, tough luck for him, I'd say. It took us long enough to get it through. There, that's something for you. That should be of interest to you.

NADA: Oh yes, and some of us are supposed to starve to death, yes? That's right, sir, gorgeous sir, we'll simply starve to death. You're kidding!

FANT: Cross my heart. Nothing but the truth. What's supposed to happen to you? Dear friend, I can't concern myself with everything. Where would I end up? Oh, I see, you've got competition over there. You know what? I think I'll try a different drummer. Is she any good?

FRANCES: Now just don't you think I'm gonna flatter you, sir.

FANT: Oh really? So what's your line then?

FRANCES: Private homes.

FANT: So you're a visiting flatterer now.

FRANCES: I'm no flatterer. I'm there for the sick. I work in homes. I make good money. (*Very secretively.*) Listen, I can be honest with you, I know. I save all my money for my brother, the porter. You must've known my brother.

FANT: The porter, of course. But he passed away.

FRANCES: He hasn't passed away.

FANT: Of course he's passed away. What do you know?

FRANCES: He hasn't passed away. I know it from a very reliable source. He's old, that's all. That's no crime. You'll be old some day!

FANT: Well, I can even show you my source. That old fogey over there has known your brother very well. He's the one who told me that he passed away. Why don't you ask him yourself.

FRANCES: Him? You can't believe a word he says. That's a flatterer! A flatterer, young man! I'll tell him to his face if you want me to. I ain't scared. Not of him. That flatterer! (*She walks toward Frankie.*) Flatterer! Flatterer! They should hang you! Hang you!

NADA: What're you doin' here? That's my spot!

FRANCES: Your spot! Your spot! I don't need your spot! What're you doin' in your spot, huh? Now you listen to me young man: he's standing there in his spot and he flatters!

NADA: Look who's talking! I'd shut up if I was you. You know what she's doin', sir? She goes door to door, with a mirror! She's got a mirror!

FRANCES: Flatterer! Flatterer! They should hang you! Hang you!

NADA: Why don't you show 'im where you keep your shard! Go ahead! Why don't you!

FANT: Keep going! Keep going! Devour each other! Fabulous!

SHAKEE: (*Appears.*) Poor old granny! Aha! (*He walks toward Frances and grabs her.*) You're under arrest.

FRANCES: He's the one you wanna grab, sir, he's a flatterer. That's his spot. That's where he flatters! I know 'im. I've watched 'im. Flatterer! Flatterer! They should hang you! Hang you!

FANT: I'll take care of him, boss. If you permit me. It'll be my pleasure.

SHAKEE: Take him away!

FANT: You've been caught in the act. Now you'll have coming what you've been asking for.

NADA: But I didn't do nothin', sir, gorgeous sir! I'm innocent. I didn't do nothin', sir, gorgeous sir.

FANT: You're flattering again. Twice in a row you said "gorgeous." Unfortunately, you're forcing me to testify against you.

NADA: What's gonna happen to me, sir, gorgeous sir? I'm innocent, really, sir, gorgeous . . .

FANT: You'll be hung. And I can't help you at all. You should've thought about that before.

NADA: (*Screaming.*) How about her? Nothing's gonna happen to her! She goes door to door! She's got a mirror!

SHAKEE: You let me worry about her. (*To Frances.*) Give me the shard!

(*François Fant takes the old man away. His moaning can be heard for a long time.*)

FRANCES: Don't you remember me, young man, sir? I'm the one who cured you. And you were sick alright, believe me. You can't imagine how sick you were. The young miss knows how sick you were, the young lady, your bride, in your room. If I hadn't cured you, you'd still be sick!

SHAKEE: So you admit that you're in possession of a shard. You're engaged in an illegal business.

FRANCES: That's because I have a brother, young man, sir, and I have to take care of him. It's for my brother. I can't let him starve to death in his old age. He was a porter.

SHAKEE: I know everything. You've been previously convicted. You had been sentenced to five years in jail for taking photographs. It was I who caught you and I personally brought you to the police. And I'll do so again today. Your previous conviction will result in heavier punishment.

FRANCES: (*Drops the shard.*) But I don't have a shard, young man, sir.

SHAKEE: You just dropped a shard. Do you think I'm blind, huh? But I will make an exception this one time. Just get out of here, quickly. If I run into you again, you're finished.
FRANCES: Thank you so much, young man, sir, thank you very much. What a kind, dear, noble young gentleman. (*She hobbles off as fast as she can. Her exclamations of gratitude merge with her brother's moaning.*)
SHAKEE: (*Picks up the mirror, everything about him indicating the greatest disgust.*) Yuk! W-w-what s-should h-happen w-with th-this? (*He is stammering again.*)

A HUGE BATHROOM

(*White tiles. The tub is sunk in the ground so that nothing breaks the evenness of the tiled surface. Killoff, who just stepped out of the tub stands there, alone, in his white robe conversing with his skin, which he rubs dry with great tenderness and care.*)

KILLOFF: I'll say it till I die. A man stands up for it. That's faith. Virility. I ask you: what's left of man today? And what really is a man, a human being? Man is his own image! What did you say? Shhh! Shut up! His own image. Yes. And without his own image, man amounts to nothing. The newspapers are filled with blood. Some news! One tragedy after the other. It never just rains, it always pours. Someone cuts his veins, another bleeds to death. Blood of the innocent. Red blood. And always blood of the young. Crying to heaven. I mean, really. Blood is red juice. All right, gentlemen, let's call it juice. But what do we do without that juice? We die! What did you say? Shhh! Shut up! We die! I might even illustrate my point with an example. How'd you like that? That'll surprise some people! When it comes to blood I draw the line. I've got my life-time supply of blood and I'm no fool. There may be others. But not me. So you're police? Go right ahead, sir, look for yourself. You won't find any objects in this house. Our heart's desire . . . you won't find it. But you know what you will find? You'll be surprised, sir. Have you heard about it yet? Bloody news! What did you say? Shhh! Shut up! Bloody news! Permit me to present to you yesterday's newspaper. There's a headline! Kindly take a look. Bloody Sunday. Regretfully, the weekend was marred again by heavy casualties. Ninety-eight people fell victim to a treacherous fate as they freely threw away their lives which had no more to offer to them. The mass cremation is scheduled for Wednesday. You are cordially invited by the Rescue Committee. So what good does that do them? A damp grave in the . . . What did you say? Shhh! Shut up! A damp grave in the dirt. It's now a whole hour that I've been waiting for my water! Of course! The water isn't hot enough yet. Not hot enough as usual. She better get my water! Is that so? She wouldn't think of it! Am I supposed to shave with cold water? I mean, really! So I cut myself and bleed? That's all I need, really! Blood! Me and blood! Where's my water? I want my water! Did you spill it again?

Boy, is she going to get it! Where's my water? (*Knocking at the door.*) Come in!

(*The door opens quietly. Nurse Luise, very timid, thin and pale enters with a wash basin. Both remain very serious and silent, while she puts the wash basin on the table. Then he yells at her.*)

KILLOFF: How often do I have to call you? I'm fed up! Fed up with that kind of negligence in my own house.

LUISE: I knocked four times, sir. I just went to heat it up. I beg your pardon, sir. It won't happen again.

KILLOFF: Are you trying to tell me that I haven't heard you? That's utter nonsense. I have ears. But I didn't hear a thing. I call this negligence. But I don't have time now. My time is far too precious for your nonsense. Where is . . . well, you know.

LUISE: Right away, sir, right away! (*She rushes out.*)

KILLOFF: Now we shall see if I really look like him. I might've gotten the wrong impression. That's possible. Especially in the street. So this boor comes along, no hat, no coat, shoes torn, dressed in rags, and tries to tell me that I look like him. You're wrong, sir, I tell him with my usual calm. 'Cause that's the way I am. Why should I get in a shouting match with a hoodlum. You're wrong, sir, I don't look like you at all. I mean, really. So what does he do? He gets pushy, he's asking for blood. My blood. But I can't stand blood. I'm all against wasting so much blood. We can do without all that blood. Red, red, red is all they think about. Nonsense, I say. Why should I bother with such nonsense? I fight life's miseries. No bloody Sunday for me! No, sirree! (*Suddenly in a very tender voice.*) There she is. My sweet little wifie! Atta girl! Aren't I lucky to have such a good wifie! And what has she got for her dear hubbie?

(*Luise appears in the door. With both hands she is holding what looks like an infant, wrapped obviously with the greatest care. Ever so slowly, as if she could only move one toe at a time, she sneaks up to Killoff.*)

KILLOFF: Now what have we got here? I bet, my sweet wifie's got something for her hubbie. What could it be? She won't open it. Why won't she open it? 'Cause he said she can't. Who said she can't? He said she can't. Look how nicely it is wrapped! What could be so nicely wrapped. It always must be nicely wrapped, you can't be careful enough with it. Man proposes, but God disposes. And suddenly we wonder: Where has all that beauty gone? Hurry up, give it to me. Oh, I could eat her up, my sweetheart, my little honeybun, look how nicely she's wrapped it for her big boy. Mommie's brought him something. Come now, hurry, you don't have to make such a big fuss, mm I feel like eating her, come on, hurry, honeybun! Let's see what my honeybun's got for her baby, her big boy!

(*Nurse Luise proceeds to unwrap layers of cloth until she produces a tiny mirror. During her husband's affectionate words there were occasional flashes of reflected light. He takes it with both hands, caresses it with one, then with the other. Suddenly he yells.*)

KILLOFF: What's that? A crack! The mirror's got a crack!

(*He raises his fist and drops it full force on his wife's head. She collapses. One can't tell if this is a direct result of her husband's punch or her natural condition.*)

THE STREET AT NIGHT

(*It is so quiet that the few lights seem frightening. They go out. Perhaps it is dawn. Fritz Shakee stalks in on an embarrassing mission. He frequently looks around, bends down to the ground and sniffs. His right hand is clenched to a fist. His arm hangs down, long and stiff like a stick. He uses it twice to knock on the floor. There are voices behind him. "Hold it!" "What are you doing?" "You want to deny it?" "Watch out!" "You are being watched!" "Watch it!" These voices are stuttering. He finds the spot he has been looking for, kneels down and digs a hole with his left hand. The voices around him swell into stuttering choruses. Each time he digs into the ground, his head tilts back, his fist opens briefly to reveal the flashing from a fragment of a mirror. He wants it buried way down in the earth, he digs and digs. But the voices are undermining his courage. He throws the shard into the hole and covers it with armloads of dirt. Then, chased by the voices, he rushes off. Soon the wind calms down. It is pouring. Morning dawns. The site of the buried mirror has become a puddle.*

Theresa Shriek opens up her store. Quietly she sneaks up to the puddle. Hearing a noise she crosses herself and rushes back inside her store. Millie wants to pay her mother a brief visit. Her eyes get caught by the puddle. She kneels down and hardly has time to quickly brush back her hair when she hears steps. She jumps up and runs off without visiting her mother. Wondrak comes racing down the street. He notices the puddle and grimaces scornfully. Now he looks at Theresa Shriek's store, now at the puddle, and gives the impression as if he is about to say "Damn." Instead, he only spits into the puddle and rushes off. Miss Bonnie May comes skipping along. She plans to do her shopping. She stops, transfixed, in front of the puddle with Wondrak's spit. Widow Holy appears, counting her money. Before she can finish, Anna Barass reaches out and takes all the money away from her. Only now do they recognize Miss Bonnie May in front of the puddle; she doesn't appreciate being watched and tippytoes angrily into the store. S. Bleiss enters on the way home from his after-hour business. He notices the ladies and walks in a wide circle around the puddle. Holy and Anna lock arms and turn back in despair. Life returns to the intersection. More people appear. They stare in the direction of the puddle. No one dares to approach it. It is bright daylight now.)

PART III

A LOBBY

(*With a high ceiling, its walls covered with dark red velvet. Stage left on a small platform is the box office, occupied by Emily Fant who would make a terrific advertisement for soaps or oils—everything about her sparkles and shines. With cold eyes and an indefatigable smile she inspects the long line of people in front of the box office. It is impossible to recognize their faces. The men have their hats pulled way over their faces and their coat collars turned up; the women are holding their handkerchiefs in front of their faces, some have scarves wrapped around their heads. No one says a word. Each is there all by himself. It seems as if everyone came dressed in black to buy a ticket to a funeral. There is only one couple, just about in the middle of the line: A woman with a bandana holding on tightly to a man's hand gradually manages to pull him toward the box office. Every now and then someone is adjusting his clothes. Sneezes are met with indignant silence. Wenzel Wondrak, invitingly attractive in his bright red uniform with shiny metal buttons, stands downstage right.*)

MME. FANT: I recommend Economy, sir. You'll love it.
MAN: How much is it?
MME. FANT: Twelve-sixty for Economy. I know, you'll love it.
MAN: How much is No Frills?
MME. FANT: You can also have No Frills. That's 6.40. As you wish. No one's forcing you.

MAN: Give me No Frills. Very simple. (*He quickly gets his ticket, pays and exits left.*)

MME. FANT: Next gentleman, please. Oh, pardon me madam, what can I do for you?

(*A tiny, heavily veiled lady whispers some unintelligible words into Emily Fant's face.*)

MME. FANT: No problem. Of course. Economy. Madam you don't really think . . . (*She gets her ticket, pays and exits.*) Next lady, please.

A TALL STOUT WOMAN: (*With a very masculine voice.*) I need your advice! It's never really worked for me. I'm too wide, that's why. D'you know how wide I am? You wouldn't believe how wide I am!

MME. FANT: There's nothing you can't get here. You just have to pick and choose.

WOMAN: Oh no, it's not that simple. I'm fatter than you, would you believe it?

MME. FANT: Well, I always get two tickets for myself. Preferably two in First Class.

WOMAN: You don't say! You've got to pay too? I could've sworn you'd get in free.

MME. FANT: Lady, I'm just an ordinary employee.

WOMAN: Really! I could've sworn you own the business.

A SHARP MALE VOICE IN THE BACK: Hurry up, will you!

A SOBER VOICE IN FRONT: Unbelievable!

A TOUGH VOICE: Beat it!

A FEMALE VOICE: We don't have all day!

WOMAN: All right. Why don't you give me two No Frills. The crowds are getting restless it seems.

MME. FANT: You're better off with Economy! Believe me. I have no personal gains in either case.

WOMAN: I take two No Frills. That's it. That'll do.

MME. FANT: That makes 12.80. You would've been better off with Economy. Next gentleman, please.

(*Henry Breeze, still in his coat, which he is wearing unbuttoned, undaunted by embarrassment, enters stage right and walks toward the concierge, who cheerfully steps in his way.*)

MME. FANT: (*Has noticed this and calls over to the concierge.*) It's all right Wondrak. The Professor may pass. The Professor gets Luxury with special equipment.

WONDRAK: I know, ladies and gentlemen, I know everything, I know.

(*Henry Breeze crosses through the lobby.*)

MME. FANT: How do you do, Professor. We certainly missed you yesterday. You aren't sick, I hope. Poor Professor, that would really be too bad.

BREEZE: Just a bit under the weather. (*Exits left.*)

THE MAN WITH THE SOMBER VOICE: Do we have to put up with this?

MME. FANT: I'm terribly sorry. That's the way she is. That woman in front only thinks about herself.

THE SOMBER MAN: So can we. And take our business some place else!

THE FEMALE VOICE: We don't have all day!

MME. FANT: You won't get a more efficient service anywhere. Go see for yourself. You'll be back. I assure you. What can I get you, sir?

THE SOMBER MAN: One No Frills. As a member of the Rescue Committee I get 50 percent.

MME. FANT: (*Furious.*) Three-twenty. (*The Somber Man pays and leaves.*) Next lady, please.

LADY: Too much! We certainly don't have all day.

MME. FANT: You are the lady who sneaked in last time. You have cheated our company.

LADY: What do you mean?

MME. FANT: I remember you. I recognized you right away. Would you please leave our sanitarium immediately.

LADY: Just give me one First Class, all right! Always this waiting around! I simply won't have it!

MME. FANT: One First Class, makes 25. Here you go, madam.

LADY: Well, finally. Don't put on airs with me! (*Pays and leaves.*)

MME. FANT: (*Louder.*) Wondrak, make sure that woman won't get in here again. She's already cheated us twice. The third time I caught her.

THE TOUGH MALE VOICE: What have we got police for?

(*Some laugh, but only briefly. Most of them move timidly away from each other.*)

MME. FANT: Next gentleman, please.

(*To everybody's surprise, a young boy suddenly appears in front of the box office.*)

BOY: How much is No Frills?

MME. FANT: Much more than your allowance, big shot! You better get home, but hurry, yes!

BOY: How much is Economy?

MME. FANT: Twelve-sixty. Pushy little fellow! Did your daddy send you?

BOY: I'll take First Class.

MME. FANT: You don't say! You really have that kind of money?

BOY: Exactly 25. Go ahead, count it!

MME. FANT: What can I say! A little prince. And look at his eyes . . . like glowing ebony. Makes you really want to kiss the little darling. A young prince from India, no less. Do I call you "Sir?"

BOY: Call me whatever you want, 's long as it makes you happy.

MME. FANT: I wouldn't dare! (*He gets his ticket. She is much slower when it comes to handing out First Class tickets.*) Next gentleman, please.

(*Joseph Killoff, carefully bundled up in coat and hat, enters stage right and walks toward the concierge.*)

MME. FANT: (*Notices him right away.*) Wondrak, the director may pass. The director gets Luxury with treatment.

WONDRAK: I know, ladies and gentlemen, I know everything, I know!

(*Killoff crosses left.*)

MME. FANT: Such a pleasure to see you, monsieur! So you didn't desert me after all!

KILLOFF: Let's see what happens when I'm dead.

MME. FANT: Please! My dear friend! Don't talk like that!

KILLOFF: No one lives forever, Mme. Fant. (*Exits left.*)

THE SPINDLY MAN WITH THE SHARP VOICE: Aha!

MME. FANT: May I help you, sir?

THE SPINDLY MAN: (*Blowing air through his lips.*) Phooo—

MME. FANT: I beg your pardon?

THE SPINDLY MAN: Phoo—

MME. FANT: I'm sorry, I can't understand you, sir. May I suggest First Class, perhaps?

THE SPINDLY MAN: No!

MME. FANT: Economy then? That'll be 12.60.

THE SPINDLY MAN: No.

MME. FANT: You want No Frills. You can have it! Why didn't you say so to begin with?

THE SPINDLY MAN: N-n-no!

MME. FANT: Then what is it you want, sir? There are people waiting, as you can see.

THE SPINDLY MAN: W-w-watch out!

MME. FANT: I can't afford to lose my customers because of you. We don't make that kind of money, as you probably know.

THE SPINDLY MAN: W-w-watch out! (*He turns around and crosses right to the end of the line, where he takes his place again. The people have become restless.*)

MME. FANT: You would think we're rolling in money! Oh well, we can manage without certain people.

(*The Couple has reached the box office.*)

WOMAN WITH BANDANA: (*To the Man.*) Stop fussing. Come on now. Chicken!

MAN: No! No!

WOMAN WITH BANDANA: Honeymoon, you said. What you say now? Always lies!

MME. FANT: (*Skeptically.*) Two No Frills?

WOMAN WITH BANDANA: Stop it, will you! No Frills on Honeymoon! Two Economy! Just so you know: Honeymoon!

MME. FANT: Surprise, surprise! Twenty-five twenty.

WOMAN WITH BANDANA: There. Take it! (*She pays and pulls the Man away with her.*)

MME. FANT: My pleasure. (*Over to Wondrak.*) You saw that, Wondrak?! Poor, but what a heart! We all could learn from them!

WONDRAK: (*While it is getting dark.*) I know, ladies and gentlemen! Everything! I know everything!

A RECORDING: Thank you and come again.

(*It is completely dark. One can hear shuffling as if from many feet. People are feeling their way on hands and feet. But these could be animals too. A wolf howls suddenly.*)

OUUU!

(*Others join in.*)

OU! OU!
WHAT'S THAT?
OU! OU!
QUIET! FOR GOD'S SAKE! QUIET!
I DON'T WANT TO!
I'M CHOKING!
LIGHT! LIGHT!

A RECORDING: Don't be afraid. You're safe here.

(*For a little while it is quiet, only the shuffling continues and finally gathers in one voice.*)

MOVE IT. WILL YOU. MOVE IT!
I CAN'T!
OU! OU!
SHUT UP, DAMN IT!
I'M AFRAID!
WHAT'S THAT?
OU! OU!

A RECORDING: Don't be afraid. Here you are underground.

(*The shuffling has stopped. Somebody yells:*)

I'M FALLING!
THE FLOOR!
OOOOHHH!
DON'T! DON'T!
GANGSTERS!
BE QUIET!
LIGHT! LIGHT!
OOHH! OOOHHH!

A RECORDING: Don't be afraid. You have arrived.

(*Now we hear only wolves and they howl from hunger and fear.*)

OOOOOOHHHHHHH!!! OOOOOOHHHHHH!!!

A RECORDING: Attention! Attention!

(*Bright light. About twenty people are sitting silently in a glaring hall of mirrors. Two rows of mirrors, one left, one right, are running all the way to the back where they are join- ed by a wide double door. Each mirror has a person sitting in front of it, motionlessly, hands on hips, sharp elbows pointed aggressively toward the neighbor on either side. No one is talking. No one is breathing. The air seems like glass. François Fant glides quietly from the front to the back, and back to the front. The floor and his soles are made of rubber. So is the smile with which he nods into every mirror. He greets the mirror images of his customers. Fritz Shakee sits down stage right, rigid to his heart's desire and without the op- portunity to stutter. Next to him, Kaldaun Jr., his pupil at school. He is taken care of by his mother Lya, who in turn is attended to by her personal maid, Millie. Barass, with his elbows, wards off his wife Anna on one side, Bleiss, the peddlar, on the other. Widow Holy has made herself quite uncomfortable sitting on two chairs, but she doesn't dare to move. Way upstage, Bonnie May, dressed in black. To the left of the double door the Six Young Girls. Eugene Kaldaun's neighbor is his former cook Marie. Marie, however, is trying her best to hold on to Preacher Crumb. He apparently doesn't like what he sees in the mirror and looks as if he'd prefer to escape. Next to him, Theresa Shriek acquaints herself with the devil. It seems the group is gathered in perfect harmony. However, no one is aware of it. With the exception of Marie and Preacher Crumb, who are honeymooning, no one has the slightest idea who else is in the hall. Everyone would be scared to death of his neighbor, but elbows are blind, and those moments cost a lot of money.*)

A LUXURY CABIN

(*In the same establishment. Fred Hero is shaving Killoff in front of a huge mirror.*)

HERO: Permit me to ask if the knife might possibly be hurting you?

KILLOFF: It's too early to tell. I have to think about it first.

HERO: I'm ready, here and now, to try another one.

KILLOFF: What if that other one hurts? That's all I'd need.

HERO: Oh no, sir, that never happens to me. All my knives are dull as a morgue.

KILLOFF: The morgue, really! The morgue. What's a knife got to do with a morgue?

HERO: Sorry, sir. Just a silly little pun off the top of my lowbrow head! Permit me to take it back.

KILLOFF: I don't mind you trying it. I like it when I can feel something. But I can't stand pain. I don't like the sight of blood. Blood is one thing I can't take.

HERO: Bravo! Personally, I'm also against tearing out the eyes. In this regard, you're just like me, Sir.

KILLOFF: Well, well, now, really. I mean.

HERO: That doesn't mean that I'd ever dare to compare myself with you, sir.

KILLOFF: That would take some nerve, I'd say.

HERO: Speaking of nerves. How are you feeling otherwise, sir. If I may say so, you seem a bit quiet today, sir.

KILLOFF: That's just it. I don't feel too bad as long as I'm in these halls—these sacred halls. But as soon as one sets foot outside, it's total exhaustion again. So many disappointments. It's no fun being young nowadays, that's for sure.

HERO: How can you say that, sir? You're still young. In the prime of your youth, so to speak.

KILLOFF: That's wonderful. But let me tell you, you wouldn't want my worries.

HERO: A little hanky, a little panky and everything will be all right again. I mean, really.

KILLOFF: How dare you! You go find someone else to listen to your nonsense. You get paid for your services. Who asked you what you mean! I mean, really! Besides, what does an ordinary employee know about worries?

HERO: I humbly admit, sir, I am a failure in every respect.

KILLOFF: If you've got no money, you've got no worries. How much can you possibly make? A few tips here and there, I s'ppose. So what d'you have to worry about? That's obvious. I mean, really.

HERO: Quite a lady, Mme. Fant, isn't she!

KILLOFF: That woman's got it. Every day, when I pass by, there're lines of people in front of the box office.

HERO: Oh, if you only knew, sir!

KILLOFF: If I only knew what? What do you know?

HERO: But I'm only telling you. It would cost me my head!

KILLOFF: So?

HERO: Sir, you must promise me.

KILLOFF: So?

HERO: She's selling three types of accommodation: First Class, of course, Economy nonetheless, and even No Frills. The difference in price is a hundred percent between each.

KILLOFF: That's how it should be.

HERO: Yes, sir, but the best is yet to come. Everybody's sitting in the same hall. And they've got exactly the same mirrors. Just imagine, if you please! There's one customer paying 6.40, while the person sitting next to him has paid 25. For the very same thing!

KILLOFF: And no one has noticed yet! That's impressive! Terrific woman, absolutely terrific!

HERO: That's been going on for ten years now and nobody has noticed. Ten years I've been working here and as far as I know, there was never a complaint. People come here and it's instant bliss, like in the song of happiness. Do you know the song of happiness, sir? Not everyone can be like you, sir!

KILLOFF: It certainly could never happen to me, I'd say.

HERO: Oh no, Mme. Fant would never dare! Her luxury clients, she always says, get only the best. A luxury man knows what he wants for his money. As for the rest—it's their own stupidity.

KILLOFF: Good for her. That's all I can say.

HERO: If only she wouldn't have such bad luck with her son. Monsieur Fant is a loser.

KILLOFF: Everybody has his cross to bear. What would life be without problems! Now I'm going to ask you a question. It'll surprise you, but I'm asking you nonetheless: Have you ever committed a murder? Yes or no?

HERO: To tell you the truth, sir: At least twelve every day.

KILLOFF: I'm not joking. I'm talking about myself. I mean, really!

HERO: You, sir? You couldn't even hurt a fly. Let alone a human being! Sir, you're blessed, if I may say so, with a heart of solid gold.

KILLOFF: That's true, I must say. But if someone's making life absolutely miserable for you?

HERO: Then something could happen. To everyone. But not you, sir!

KILLOFF: Baloney! Things will have to change! Everything'll have to change!

A THUNDERING VOICE: Oh yes, frivolity thy name is woman! Robbing us of the sweetest fruit! Depriving us of the hard-earned rewards for our work! (*Applause.*)

KILLOFF: He's right. I must say, he's right.

HERO: Sir, I don't understand.

KILLOFF: Just be quiet, all right!

THE THUNDERING VOICE: Who needs to roam if you can have it at home? Things can't go on like this. The world is falling apart! (*Thundering applause.*)

HERO: I don't understand why . . .

KILLOFF: Of course, these things are beyond you. It can't go on like this. The world is falling apart! Everything will have to change.

THE THUNDERING VOICE: Must we suffer for the rest of our lives the consequences of a tiny flaw? Let bygones be bygones! What we need now is the rebirth, the resurrection of our commitment to what is true and authentic, real and genuine, to purity and perfection! (*Applause.*)

HERO: Strange, how well you can hear him. I really don't know . . .

KILLOFF: Here you go again, talking about yourself. You don't interest me at all, mister!

HERO: You're so right, sir, it kills me. The shave you get is heavenly. But something's wrong with the conversation. If I may offer an advice, sir, you seem a bit quiet and depressed today. Why don't you try Luxury with Soul! You can order it right now! A most respected lady, sophisticated, elegant, a doctor, excellent family, outstanding education and does she know how to talk! People come in here, feeling down and out, but when they leave, they're innocent like newborn children.

KILLOFF: Innocent?

HERO: In a manner of speaking, I mean. Sir, do me a favor and order the lady. She comes with Luxury. I beg you. It's been a pleasure, sir, I hope you like your shave. It's been a pleasure. I'll send the lady over.

THE ADJOINING LUXURY CABIN

(*Henry Breeze stands in full view of his mirror image and speaks. The walls of his cabin are covered from top to bottom with big round holes. In his left he holds a small, handy machine with several buttons and a wire, which is plugged into the wall.*)

BREEZE: Enormous amounts of money are being thrown out, wasted every day, day after day. But the people are suffering. The people are starving! We don't want to suffer and we don't want to starve. (*He pushes a button, applause comes through the holes.*) To each his own. Aren't we all fully grown, mature adults? But what are these gentlemen like? One good turn deserves another. Stay off my turf and I'll stay off yours! Oh yes, frivolity thy name is woman! Robbing us of the sweetest fruit! Depriving us of the hard-earned rewards for our work! (*He pushes a button: applause.*) If we were girls, very young girls, we might get a kick out of this. Unfortunately, we aren't, and never will be. I say, this shady traffic in immensely profitable commodities must be stopped. This cut-throat competition in dirt-cheap discounts and specials must be wiped out once and for all. (*He pushes several times: thundering applause.*) I say, hands off such foul business! For the ending won't be happy. Believe me, there are many among us who would make terrific chairmen of any board, but they haven't got a chance today. Hate thy neighbor as thyself seems the motto of the day. (*He pushes the button: big applause.*) Now even the most handsome, the most steadfast of men have been trapped and more often than not won over by good food and loving care. Doesn't love go through the stomach? As long as we go on living, we'll keep on loving. It's always the same old forgotten song. No one alive is alone in this world. No living being can ever be all to itself. (*He pushes the button: the applause is weaker.*) Man is not a scarecrow. Not to speak of outstanding men like us! Each of us carries a noble image in his heart. When will we be able to truly claim it as our own? The British have a world-famous saying: My home is my castle . . . or: Who needs to roam if you can have it at home! (*He pushes the button: weak applause.*) It can't go on like this. The world is falling apart! (*He pushes the button: the applause is barely audible.*) Must we suffer for the rest of our lives the consequences of a tiny flaw? Let bygones be bygones! Let us join hands! No one, and I mean no one, not even the devil can tear us apart! (*He pushes the button. There is no applause. He pushes and pushes. He stamps his foot angrily. It doesn't do any good. He goes to the door and pulls the emergency alarm: a very shrill bell. Then he nervously paces his cabin, talking to himself, now very quickly and completely without pathos.*) What we need now is rebirth, the resurrection of our commitment to what is true and authentic, real and genuine, to purity and perfection. For only he who is beautiful knows what beauty is and only the strong man appreciates strength. Then the old ways, tradition, which is supposed to be dead, gone, finished will return in full glory. Do not discard the old ways. Where would we be without tradition? Honor thy father and mother. Egyptians and Babylonians, Assyrians and Persians, Greeks and Romans, mighty empires came to an end, awesome powers . . .

WONDRAK: (*Rushes in.*) What happened to the mirror?

BREEZE: Oh, there you are. Tell me, what's wrong with the applause machine? I keep pushing and pushing and nothing happens. I can't take this any longer. I'm a nervous wreck. This place makes you completely sick!

WONDRAK: How true, Professor, so true, couldn't be truer!

BREEZE: You may not believe it. But you better believe me. I'm too sensitive. I've waited a long time before I pulled the alarm. I didn't want to create extra work for you. I'm far too sensitive toward you people! Here, try it yourself.

WONDRAK: With pleasure, Professor, with pleasure. (*He pushes.*)

BREEZE: You see! It doesn't applaud. It won't applaud! Now this wall's starting. But the other one is completely dead. It may have applauded three times, four at the most. I am desperate. Could you possibly adjust it yourself?

WONDRAK: I can try, Professor, I'll give it a try, Professor, but who knows, who can tell if it will do any good?

BREEZE: Don't you have an emergency unit? That really is inexcusable. An institution like this and no emergency unit! You can tell Mme. Fant that I'm truly upset. I've been coming now for ten years, every day. You couldn't have a better customer. Oh well, there's the director, who keeps ıuıınıng into me in the lobby but he doesn't count. Tell Mme. Fant that I couldn't be angrier! I'll give her five minutes to fix this machine! I don't know what I'll be capable of doing if it doesn't work by then! I couldn't be angrier!

WONDRAK: Very true, Professor, couldn't be truer! (*He rushes out.*)

LIGHT IN THE ADJOINING CABIN

LEDA FRESH-BREEZE: I'm afraid you think too much, director. Just relax for a minute. Let go of all tensions. I know you have a lot of important things to think about. A man in your position! Such responsibility! It's very understandable! No one's going to hold it against you. That's understood. That's to be expected in your case. But if you want to do me a favor, a special favor, just for me—you did say that you find me likable—then try and let go completely, just for once, don't think of anything. Just rest. Wait, perhaps you should sit this way. (*She turns around his chair so that he turns his back to the mirror.*)

KILLOFF: Wouldn't that be nice . . . to be able to relax for once.

LEDA: How's that? Are you comfortable? I think you are. Now just tell me anything that's going through your mind.

KILLOFF: Oh, if that were so easy, madam.

LEDA: I'll help you. That's my job. Just think back, when you were a boy, a big boy already, and you did something bad, something really bad and you were so afraid of your daddy, in fact sometimes you hated your father so much that you'd go to your mommie and put your head on her shoulder and confess.

KILLOFF: (*Swallowing.*) The big boy, that was me all right, I've always been the big boy.

LEDA: You see, I've known this all along and I don't even know you! You'll find out how much I know. You can tell me everything that's going through your head. I know it anyway, regardless of whether you tell me or not. It'll just go faster if you do the talking.

KILLOFF: My wife has passed away. That's what I am thinking about.

LEDA: There! You see. I knew that and I also knew why you've been so sad.

KILLOFF: What do you expect, when my wife has died! Isn't this reason to be sad!

LEDA: You listen to me, big boy. It's not your fault that your wife died. We all must die. It's a law of nature. The laws of nature are eternal. It's not your fault, don't you see! If it were your fault, the situation would be different, but I know everything and I also know that it's not your fault.

KILLOFF: Of course it's not my fault.

LEDA: If it were your fault, you'd be a murderer. Is this the face of a murderer? Seriously now, turn around and take a good look in the mirror. Is this the face of a murderer? Yes or no? If you disagree, if you should feel that this could indeed be the face of a murderer, don't hesitate to say so. I won't be angry with you, we can't always agree, can we. As far as I'm concerned I could swear that this could never be the face of a murderer.

KILLOFF: You're absolutely right.

LEDA: You'll find out that I'm always right. Do you know what I just found out? I'll tell you to your face. Don't get scared, I'll have to tell you. Try and stay calm. It's not that bad.

KILLOFF: Why? Why should I? My conscience is clean.

LEDA: Nonetheless, I'll tell you straight to your face: You don't like looking in the mirror!

KILLOFF: (*Gasping for air.*) Yes . . . no . . . I mean, really!

LEDA: Calm down! I'm not after you. I'm not an investigator. I am a doctor. A female doctor, to be precise.

KILLOFF: That really is too much! That . . . reminds me that it's time for me to go now.

LEDA: (*Pushes him down in his chair.*) Not yet! It's not time yet, silly! Such a big boy and so mistrustful! It's not a sin and it's not a crime either. No man is obligated to enjoy looking in the mirror. Yes, it is a natural law that man likes doing it, but there are always the exceptions to prove the rules. Why shouldn't you be the exception? You are not vain. What's wrong with that?

KILLOFF: There you are. There's nothing wrong with it.

LEDA: At present, you are not vain. You don't feel like seeing yourself in your present condition. It used to be different, of course. You used to enjoy mirrors, like every other normal person. Forgive me for using this banned word so much. You might consider it indecent. There's something in your resisting anyone—and particularly a woman—who uses this kind of word. But it is my job to cure you. That's all I care about. It is in your own interest that I have to just go ahead and call the most disgusting things by their real names.

KILLOFF: Disgusting it is. You can say that again!

LEDA: You see. I even know that you find all this disgusting. Now that we've agreed on this, we can go on. So you don't like looking in the mirror. Do you realize that you even blushed just now?

KILLOFF: That's possible. One does get embarrassed at times, you know.

LEDA: You're beginning to get scared of me, because I know everything. Now listen to me carefully. You don't have to be scared. Don't you see that the fact that you don't like looking in the mirror speaks only for your decency! You are inhibited. But these inhibitions can be overcome. Since your wife is dead, you don't want to have anything to do with mirrors. That doesn't keep you from coming to our sanitarium. Some dark force inside you makes you come here. But as soon as you see a mirror, you turn away, filled with hatred. Am I right?

KILLOFF: Yes. I don't like it . . . Mirrors.

LEDA: Since your wife's death something has broken.

KILLOFF: (*Yells.*) You're so right!!

LEDA: Don't be misled by a delusion! We can't always trust our memory. Often we confuse the effect with the cause. Right now you have the feeling that everything has already happened much earlier; that even while your wife was still alive you couldn't find enjoyment in anything. That the mirror, the arch-image of all human joys—oh yes, that's the way it is, there's nothing I can do about that—in any case, you have the impression that the mirror has broken first and your wife died afterwards. You're afraid that you are partly responsible for the death of your wife, because the tragedy with the mirror happened before that. But that is not the way it was. Believe me! Everything you think about it is wrong. FIRST your wife died and THEN the mirror broke.

KILLOFF: That's right! You're so right!

LEDA: You see! You're absolutely innocent! It's not your fault. It's never been your fault.

THUNDERING VOICE: One good turn deserves another. Stay off my turf and I'll stay off yours!

KILLOFF: I mean, really!

LEDA: Don't let him bother you. It's my husband.

KILLOFF: What does he want now?

LEDA: Something seems to be wrong again with the applause machine. It's only my husband. Don't let him bother you. Let's just go on.

THUNDERING VOICE: Enormous amounts of money are being thrown out, wasted, every day, day after day. But the people are suffering. The people are starving.

KILLOFF: He should first get dry behind his ears! A kid like him, what does he know about economics!

LEDA: Don't pay any attention to him. It's just my husband. Can you imagine what this luxury cabin with special equipment costs me every day? I better not tell you. But let's go on.

KILLOFF: You can't even hear your own voice!

THUNDERING VOICE: Believe me, there are many among us who would make terrific chairmen of any board, but they haven't got a chance today. Hate thy neighbor like thyself seems the motto of the day. No one alive is alone in this world. No living being can ever be all to itself. Honor thy father and mother. Egyptians and Babylonians, Assyrians and Persians, Greeks and Romans . . .

LEDA: I can't figure it out. That doesn't come from the cabin next to us. He's walking around in the hallway. He can't do that. It interferes with the entire program.

KILLOFF: I've never seen such chutzpah! You better teach that boy some manners. I'm not about to put up with this! At those prices!

MME. FANT: (*Comes rushing in.*) For God's sake, doctor, help me! Your husband's gone crazy! He's having a fit! A madman, in my sanitarium! A madman!

KILLOFF: Let me ask you, Madame Fant, do we get luxury or not?

MME. FANT: For God's sake, of course, sir! I don't know where to begin, he's ruining my establishment, I'm afraid he'll start smashing my mirrors, my child isn't here, I've got no man to help me. Just work, work, work, day and night, night and day, day and night. Doctor, I implore you, do something about him, doctor, I beg you, help me. Oh my friend, I give you anything you want before he starts attacking my mirrors! It's going to be a catastrophe, a catastrophe!

KILLOFF: Let me take care of him. That boy's going to get it. It's not my style but now it's going to be my style. I'll smash in his teeth! Bastard! You know what I'd call him? Inconsiderate!

LEDA: That's how he always is. That's how he is. My husband—inconsiderate.

MME. FANT: My child! Where is my child? Come, help your mother, child!

(*All three of them rush out into the hallway.*)

(*Nothing has changed in the Hall of Mirrors. The same people are sitting there, quietly, eyes fixed at their mirror image. François Fant is pacing up and down without making the slightest noise. Suddenly, a raging voice can be heard, at first from afar, but it is rapidly approaching.*)

RAGING VOICE: To each his own! Aren't we all fully grown, mature adults? (*Kaldaun Jr. recoils.*) Oh yes, frivolity, thy name is woman! Robbing us of the sweetest fruit! Depriving us of the hard-earned rewards for our work! (*Barass recoils.*) If we were young girls, very young girls, we might get a kick out of this. Unfortunately, we are not and we will never be! (*The Six Girls recoil.*) I say, this shady traffic in immensely profitable commodities must be stopped. This cut-throat competition in dirt-cheap discounts and specials must be wiped out once and for all! (*S. Bleiss recoils.*) Believe me, there are many among us who would make terrific chairmen of any board, but they haven't got a chance today. Hate thy neighbor as thyself seems the motto of the day. (*Shakee recoils.*) Even the most handsome, the most steadfast of men have been trapped and more often than not won over by good food and loving care. (*Miss Bonnie May recoils.*) Doesn't love go through the stomach? As long as we go on living, we keep on loving. (*Widow Holy recoils.*) It's always the same old forgotten song. (*Eugene Kaldaun recoils.*) No one alive is alone in this world. No living being can ever be all to itself. (*Marie and Preacher Crumb recoil toward each other.*) Man is not a scarecrow. Not to speak of outstanding men like us! (*Barass recoils more vigorously.*) Each of us carries a noble image in his heart. When will we be able to truly claim it as our own? (*Lya Kaldaun recoils.*) The British have a world-famous saying: My home is my castle. Who needs to roam if you can have it at home! It can't go on like this. The world is falling apart! Must we suffer all our lives the consequences of a tiny flaw? (*Millie Shriek recoils.*) What we need now is the rebirth, the resurrection of our commitment to what is true and authentic, real and genuine, to purity and perfection. For only he who is beautiful knows what beauty is (*François Fant recoils and listens*) and only the strong man appreciates strength! (*Barass raises both hands and grabs his mirror.*) Then the old ways, tradition, which is supposed to be dead, gone, finished, will return in full glory. Do not discard the old ways! (*Anna Barass recoils.*) Where would we be without tradition? Honor thy father and mother!

(*François Fant exits. He leaves the double door open, which offers a view of endless halls of mirrors.*)

RAGING VOICE: Egyptians and Babylonians, Assyrians and Persians, Greeks and Romans, mighty empires came to an end, awesome powers! Up to the present day every civilization perished from its own ingratitude. Think of our parents, our predecessors and ancestors, were their lives wasted or worse yet, have they lived *in vain*? Centuries, millenia, billenia are looking down on us, watching us! The French, never far behind the British, also have a saying: qui vivra, verra. Man better keep his eyes open! (*Everyone recoiling, twitching, quivering, agitated.*) We won't have this right taken away from us! And we certainly won't let ourselves be stripped! Is it the past or is it the future that is challenging, testing us, demanding that we stand up for ourselves? I propose: Both! Both challenge us, demanding from us that we remember once again where we are coming from and to remind ourselves where we are going to! Let us join hands!

(*Everyone thrusts out his arms. Everyone grabs a mirror and tears it from the wall. Everyone jumps up, screaming:*)

I! I! I! I! I! I! I! I! I! I! I! I! I! I!

(*With their mirrors raised high they rush to the front. Killoff and Mme. Fant enter stage right imploring the crowd, trying to stand in their way. Their words cannot be heard in the noise. They are being run over and remain lying on the floor. The crowd pushes out stage right. There are many more pushing their way out from the galleries in the back. The mirrorless walls collapse and we are back:*)

IN THE STREET

(*A black stream is moving down the street. People join in from all sides. Everyone is hold-*

ing a mirror or a picture of himself high up in the air. The air is reverberating with thunderous shouts of I! I! I! I! I! I! But they never merge into a real chorus. Slowing rising in the back is the monument of Henry Breeze.)

END

LIFE-TERMS

CHARACTERS

Fifty
The Friend
Locketeer
One Man
Another
Mother, 32
Boy, 70
Man, Professor, 46
Woman, 43
Grandmother
Granddaughter
Young Ten
Two Colleagues
The Couple
Young Woman at the Funeral of her Child
Two Young Men, 28 and 88
Two Ladies
Chorus of the Unequal
Two Very Old Women, 93 and 96

PROLOGUE ABOUT THE OLD TIMES

ONE MAN: Back then!

ANOTHER: Back when? You really believe in that old wives' tale!

ONE: But that's how it was. Just take a look at some of the eyewitness reports!

ANOTHER: Did you actually read them?

ONE: Of course. That's why I'm telling you.

ANOTHER: So what did they say?

ONE: Just what I told you. A man leaves his house to buy cigarettes. He says to his wife, "I'll be back in a few minutes. I'll be right back." He steps outside and wants to cross the street, the store is right there. Suddenly a car comes around the corner and runs him over. He's lying in the street. Multiple fractures of the skull.

ANOTHER: So? What happened then? They took him to the hospital and cured him. He was hospitalized for several weeks.

ONE: No. He was dead.

ANOTHER: Dead. It was his *moment*.

ONE: It wasn't. That's just the point. That's what I've been trying to tell you.

ANOTHER: What was his name?

ONE: Peter Paul.

ANOTHER: But what was his real name?

ONE: Peter Paul.

ANOTHER: Yeah! That's what they're always trying to tell me. Do you really believe that back then people could actually live without a proper name?

ONE: I'm telling you. That's how it was. People had any old names and those names meant nothing.

ANOTHER: Then you could've even changed your name.

ONE: Of course. It didn't matter what you were called.

ANOTHER: And the name had nothing to do with the *moment*?

ONE: Absolutely nothing. The *moment* was unknown.

ANOTHER: I don't understand. Are you trying to tell me that no one, absolutely no one had any idea when the moment of his death would be?

ONE: Exactly. No one knew.

ANOTHER: Now tell me, seriously: can you imagine what that was like?

ONE: To tell you the truth: No. That's why I find it so interesting.

ANOTHER: But how could they've been able to stand it! The uncertainty! The fear! It would have driven me out of my mind! I wouldn't have been able to think of anything else. How did these people live? If they couldn't even step outside! How could they plan anything? How could they *look forward* to anything? I find it horrible.

ONE: That it was. I can't figure it either.

ANOTHER: But do you *believe* it? Do you *believe* that's how it was?

ONE: That's why one studies history.

ANOTHER: You mean mythology . . . I'm willing to believe that there were cannibals . . .

ONE: And pygmies . . .

ANOTHER: And giants, witches, mastodonts and mammoths, but this is an entirely different matter.

ONE: What other proofs do you want me to give you?

ANOTHER: Maybe I never really thought about it carefully enough. It sounds *ghastly*. Unbelieveable.

ONE: And yet life did go on.

ANOTHER: Maybe people were more stupid then. Stupefied.

ONE: You mean, like animals. They don't think either.

ANOTHER: Yes. They just hunt, eat and play and never stop to think about what could happen to them.

ONE: I'd say we have advanced a bit.

ANOTHER: A bit? Whatever came before could hardly be called human!

ONE: And yet people painted and wrote and made music. They had their philosophers and great minds.

ANOTHER: That's ridiculous. Today every little shoemaker is a greater philosopher, because he knows what's going to happen to him. He is able to organize his life in every detail, down to the last minute. He can make plans without fear, he is absolutely certain of his term in life. He can count on the number of his years as surely as he can count his toes and fingers.

ONE: I think the discovery of the *moment* represents the greatest progress in human history.

ANOTHER: What came before were savages, that's all. Poor bastards.

ONE: Animals.

PART I

MOTHER AND BOY

(*A mother is running after her little boy.*)

MOTHER: Seventy! Seventy! Where are you?

BOY: You'll never catch up with me, Mom!

MOTHER: And you always have to make me lose my breath!

BOY: You love running after me, Mom!

MOTHER: And you love to make me run, bad boy! Where are you now?

BOY: Up in the tree! Where you can't catch me!

MOTHER: You come down right now! You're going to fall down. The branches are brittle.

BOY: And why shouldn't I fall, Mom?

MOTHER: You'll hurt yourself.

BOY: So what, Mom? Why shouldn't I hurt myself? A brave boy isn't afraid of pain.

MOTHER: Sure. Sure. But something might happen to you.

BOY: Nothing will happen to me, not me. My name is Seventy.

MOTHER: One never knows. It's better to be careful.

BOY: But Mom, it was you who explained it all to me.

MOTHER: What did I explain to you?

BOY: You told me that my name is Seventy because I am going to live seventy years. You said you're called Thirty-two, because you'll have to die at the age of thirty-two.

MOTHER: Yes. Yes. But you might break a leg.

BOY: May I ask you something, Mom?

MOTHER: Anything, my son, anything.

BOY: Do you really have to die when you're thirty-two?

MOTHER: Yes, of course, my child. I've explained all that to you.

BOY: Mom, do you know what I've figured out?

MOTHER: What, my child?

BOY: I'll be living thirty-eight years longer than you.

MOTHER: Thank God, my child.

BOY: Mom, how many more years are you going to live?

MOTHER: That's too sad. Why do you ask?

BOY: But you'll be living many more years, right, Mom?

MOTHER: Not too many.

BOY: How many, Mom? I want to know how many.

MOTHER: That's a secret, my child.

BOY: Does Dad know?

MOTHER: No.

BOY: Does Granddad know?

MOTHER: No.

BOY: Does Grandma know?

MOTHER: No.

BOY: Does the teacher know?

MOTHER: No.

BOY: No one knows? No one in the whole wide world?

MTOHER: No one. No one knows.

BOY: Oh Mom, I want to know!

MOTHER: Why do you torture me? What good would it do if you knew?

BOY: I have to know.

MOTHER: But why? Why?

BOY: I'm so scared, Mom. Everyone says you'll die young. I want to know how much longer you'll be running after me, because I love you so much. I'm scared, Mom.

MOTHER: You mustn't be scared. You'll grow up to be a successful, decent man, you'll have a wife and many children and even more grandchildren. You'll live to be old, seventy, and when you die, there'll already be great-grandchildren.

BOY: But I don't like them. I only like you. Tell me, Mom.

MOTHER: Don't be so stubborn. I can't tell you.

BOY: You don't like me.

MOTHER: I like you more than anyone else. You know that.

BOY: Mom, I won't be able to sleep if you don't tell me.

MOTHER: You're terrible. You've been sleeping all right so far.

BOY: That's what you think. That's what you think. I'm only pretending. As soon as you leave the room I'm opening my eyes and I look at the ceiling. That's when I'm counting the circles.

MOTHER: What for? You should be sleeping instead.

BOY: But those are the good-night kisses I'll still be getting from you. I count them, I count them every night, but they never come out right. Sometimes there are so many, sometimes there are just a few—I never see the same number of circles, you know. I want to know how many there are. Otherwise I'll never be able to fall asleep again.

MOTHER: I'm going to tell you, my child. You'll still be getting more than a hundred good-night kisses from me.

BOY: More than a hundred! More than a hundred! Oh Mom, now I'll be able to sleep. . . .

FIFTY AND FRIEND

FIFTY: The best age? I don't think so.

FRIEND: But up to now it's always been right.

FIFTY: I don't believe it. And I can easily prove to you just the opposite. You say that everyone has his *moment* just at the right time. Give me one example.

FRIEND: I only have to think of my own family. My father's name was Sixty-three. That's exactly how old he was when it happened. My mother belongs to the fortunate ones. She's still alive.

FIFTY: What's your mother's name?

FRIEND: Ninety-six.

FIFTY: She couldn't be that old. That's true. But that doesn't mean . . .

FRIEND: Wait. Wait. I want to tell you something. I had a little sister. She was very special. We were all in love with her. She had long curly hair and beautiful dark eyelashes. It was enchanting to watch her opening her eyes. She'd do it very slowly and her eyelashes were like quiet wings lifting you way up and as you began to feel lighter and lighter—and that's what was so strange—you'd also be lying in the shadow of her feet.

FIFTY: You speak like a man in love.

FRIEND: She was a child. I wasn't the only one who worshipped her. Everyone who met her was touched by her angelic beauty.

FIFTY: And what became of her?

FRIEND: She's no longer alive. She died a very young girl.

FIFTY: What was her name?

FRIEND: Her name was Twelve.

FIFTY: You never told me about her.

FRIEND: I never talk about her. I've never gotten over it.

FIFTY: *Did she know?*

FRIEND: We've thought about that a lot. It's not easy to keep these things secret from a young girl. They are curious and they eavesdrop on the conversations of the adults.

FIFTY: True. They're all obsessed with the meaning of their names. All children are. The way they keep tormenting their mothers until they confess everything to them!

FIFTY: But my sister was different. She never asked any questions. Maybe she had a premonition that her *moment* would come soon, but if she did, she never let anyone know. She was such a calm, even-tempered child. She could never be rushed. If she was told, "You'll be late for school," she'd say, "I've time. I'll get there on time." And even though she was so slow, she was never late.

FIFTY: That sounds amazingly well-balanced for a child her age.

FRIEND: That's just it. We didn't understand it. She never got into a fight. She never took anything from another child. She had no special wishes. She was happy about everything she discovered and she'd look at it for a long time, slowly, with her special intensity. Looking back it seems to me that *observing* meant everything to her. It gave her happiness. She'd study things for a long time the way others would *love*.

FIFTY: I would've liked to have seen her.

FRIEND: Oh, that was a long time ago. Over thirty years.

FIFTY: We didn't even know each other then. She must have been very ill.

FRIEND: Of course. But let's not talk about that now. I'm not telling you this just for the hell of it. I am telling you what she was called so you know that that was exactly what happened to her.

FIFTY: I don't doubt your words.

FRIEND: How could you? You'd hurt me very deeply. How could I lie about this?

FIFTY: Of course you couldn't. It's all much too serious. Still, I want to ask you something.

FRIEND: Yes?

FIFTY: You'll be surprised how ignorant I am, but until today I have refused to find out more about our repulsive customs.

FRIEND: There isn't as much to find out as you may think.

FIFTY: Wait. Wait. I'll surprise you yet. But for now just tell me this: have you ever known a person who confessed his age to you?

FRIEND: I don't understand. What do you mean?

FIFTY: Exactly what I've been saying. Has anyone ever told you his real age?

FRIEND: Someone who's still alive?

FIFTY: Who else? Someone who's no longer alive wouldn't be able to tell you.

FRIEND: If I didn't know you better, I'd say you're retarded, a born moron, a hopeless vegetable.

FIFTY: That's why I'm asking you. I've never dared to ask anyone this question.

FRIEND: And that's why you're asking me.

FIFTY: Yes. Confidentially. You won't tell on me.

FRIEND: If I did, they would lock you up or commit you to the loonie bin.

FIFTY: All right! All right! Answer my question and don't worry about the loonie bin. I'm asking you again: Did anyone ever confess his age to you?

FRIEND: No, of course not. Nobody does that. It wouldn't even occur to any-one that one can do such a thing. The worst bastard wouldn't stoop that low.

FIFTY: Fine. Let's keep that in mind, please. You don't know anyone who's ever done it. No one says how old he is.

FRIEND: No. No one. But what are you trying to get at?

FIFTY: How does one know that the *moment* is indeed the right one? Perhaps this is just a superstition.

FRIEND: (*Laughs out loud.*) You don't know that? You really don't know? You don't know the first thing that happens when someone dies? First, the event of death has to be officially pronounced by the appropriate authority in front of witnesses. Only then can the locket be opened.

FIFTY: What locket?

FRIEND: Where have you been?! The locket which you carry around your neck. You've always been carrying it, since your birth. It is sealed in such a way that nobody can open it. The locketeer or coroner is the only one who can.

FIFTY: You mean this? (*He pulls a small locket from under his shirt and holds it up to the Friend.*) This silly thing?

FRIEND: Don't be naughty now. Yes, I mean this silly thing.

FIFTY: I never knew what it was good for. I remember ever since I was a little child they kept telling me that I must take very good care of it. My mother always used to threaten me. She'd say that if I'd ever lose it or anything would happen to it I would have to starve to death.

FRIEND: She was right. But in a different way than you could have grasped at that time.

FIFTY: I took the whole thing for an old wives' tale.

FRIEND: But you never tried to open the locket?

FIFTY: No. Just as I never tried to open up my chest.

FRIEND: You were a good child. I'm glad you stayed that way.

FIFTY: And what if I'd have opened it? What was there to find anyway?

FRIEND: The exact day of your birth. The exact year of your death. Nothing else. The locket is put around the child's neck immediately after the birth ceremony and no one ever touches it again until the coroner or locketeer takes it again.

FIFTY: And that's accepted as sufficient proof?

FRIEND: It *is* proof. Because as soon as the child is able to talk and understand, he is told by his mother how old he is. And he is threatened with the heavi-est punishment should he ever dare to give away his age. Don't try to tell me now that you don't remember.

FIFTY: Yes. Yes. I've heard something about having a birthday, I think . . .

FRIEND: Now, if the locket shows the same birthday they've told you about and if one dies on the same day—isn't that proof enough?

FIFTY: It proves that man dies on his birthday. But couldn't it be out of fear of his birthday . . . ?

FRIEND: But he also knows himself how old he is. And the locket is proof of it, don't you see! It contains the year of his death.

FIFTY: You haven't convinced me. The dead man doesn't say anything. And the locketeer could be lying.

FRIEND: The locketeer? How could he? He had been sworn into his office! And the only purpose of his position is to read and reveal the contents of the locket.

FIFTY: He could have been sworn into an official lie.

COURTSHIP

MAN: You look familiar.

WOMAN: I've seen you many times.

MAN: If I only knew where I've seen you before.

WOMAN: Keep thinking! You might remember.

MAN: I'm racking my brains.

WOMAN: But you don't remember.

MAN: I'm so sorry. I don't like being impolite.

WOMAN: Oh you aren't. On the contrary! Shall I give you a hint?

MAN: That would be very kind.

WOMAN: You're Professor Forty-six.

MAN: That's right! You even know my name!

WOMAN: I know it and respect it.

MAN: It's you! Now I remember! You're the lady in the first row!

WOMAN: Could be. Keep guessing!

MAN: No, no, it's you! You're always sitting in the first row. I recognize your eyes. You're always looking at me so strangely. I don't know what it is, but your eyes are hard to forget.

WOMAN: I thought you didn't even notice me. You always seem so concentrated.

MAN: I am. I am. But I've been noticing your eyes for a long time. One other thing . . .

WOMAN: What is it?

MAN: I really don't know you otherwise. Would you be kind enough to tell me your name?

WOMAN: My name is Forty-three.

MAN: Forty-three? We're very close then.

WOMAN: I've known that for a long time, Professor Forty-six.

MAN: Tell me, do you also pay such great attention to this kind of thing?

WOMAN: The greatest! That was the reason why I always sat in the first row.

MAN: So you came only because of my name?

WOMAN: Yes. But then I came back.

MAN: And still because of my name?

WOMAN: Yes.

MAN: You weren't disappointed?

WOMAN: Oh no. I simply had to see you again.

MAN: Did you ever listen to what I was saying?

WOMAN: Yes. I also listened. But I must admit, I was thinking mostly about you.

MAN: About me? What's there to think about?

WOMAN: Your destiny. It became an obsession with me. How much longer will he be able to speak like that? How much longer? How much longer? I couldn't think of anything else.—Now I've said it. Now you'll despise me.

MAN: Are you always like that? Obsessed with such thoughts?

WOMAN: Oh no! I only had them while I was sitting in front of you.

MAN: That surprises me. There certainly is nothing special about my name. On the contrary, I always had to suffer from my somewhat mediocre name.

WOMAN: Oh I know. I know what you're talking about.

MAN: And you were never interested in high-class young men?

WOMAN: You mean, in young Eighty-eighters?

MAN: Yes—really high ones.

WOMAN: No. I never could stand those. Eighty-eighters are so full of themselves and they're so stupid. I knew one, who wouldn't even say hello to me. He has been introduced to me repeatedly over the years, but he hasn't said hello to me once. I don't like that kind of arrogance.

MAN: Well, there are so few of them . . . but you must have felt differently as a young girl. They must have impressed you then.

WOMAN: Never! Believe me. Never. I could never understand the other girls. What has that kind of man accomplished? He gets his eighty-eight years put around his neck at birth and that's it. He doesn't have to do anything but show off his name and have a good time. Everything else comes his way all by itself.

MAN: That's true.

WOMAN: I don't like easy-going men. I like people who have it *hard* with their names. A man like you thinks. You *have* to think, otherwise you won't accomplish anything.

MAN: But an Eighty-eighter would have so much more time. Just imagine the things he could do if he'd only want to.

WOMAN: I don't think so. They're all heartless. They *have to* be heartless.

MAN: But why?

WOMAN: To begin with, because that kind of man knows for sure: he will survive everyone who is close to him. Not only his parents and the older generation—that would be natural; but he'll also survive his brothers and sisters, his friends, colleagues, his wives and, in most cases, even his children. That's what he's telling himself from the very start. How could he love anyone? How could he get attached to anyone? He doesn't know pity, he can't help anyone. His years belong to him alone. He can't give them away. But he wouldn't want to, anyway. Because he has become tough, as if nothing else existed besides him. And for this he is admired! I detest Eighty-eighters! I hate Eighty-eighters!

MAN: You are an unusual woman.

WOMAN: Perhaps I am. I don't want to survive the man I love. But I don't want him to survive me either. And that's not just jealousy, as you may think.

MAN: No. That's a very healthy attitude.

WOMAN: A couple shoud start out together and end up together. I've sworn to myself: I am not going to marry a man who'll die right in front of my eyes. But by the same token, neither will I marry one who's going to watch me die. It *disgusts* me too much, you know.

MAN: You just want to be doubly sure. It isn't enough for you to know what you are all about.

WOMAN: No. I want to know my husband as well as I know myself.

MAN: What you are looking for, if I may say so, is the *joint moment*.

WOMAN: The *joint moment*.

MAN: That's why you're sitting in the first row.

WOMAN: Yes.

MAN: Will you always be sitting in the first row?

WOMAN: Yes.

MAN: Even when you know for sure?

WOMAN: Yes.

MAN: Even when you are his wife?

WOMAN: Yes!

MAN: With the same look in your eyes?

WOMAN: Yes! Yes!

FIFTY AND THE LOCKETEER

LOCKETEER: I look at every single one. That's what I've been authorized to do. There must be no abuse. The continued existence and safety of our society depends on everyone having to observe his *moment*. I call it the contract. At birth, everyone gets this contract around his neck. We grow up with, we live among our fellow-men. We don't mind all the advantages of life in a community. Not everyone deserves these advantages. But we have so many years assigned to us and they can't be changed.

FIFTY: Don't you ever have accidents? What if someone gets into a train accident *before* his *moment*?

LOCKETEER: Then nothing will happen to him.

FIFTY: How does that work?

LOCKETEER: That is the function of my office. You have interrupted my presentation. How do you want to get to the bottom of the truth, if you can't listen?

FIFTY: I'm a little impatient. This is a very exciting question. You must excuse my impatience, but I am extremely excited by this question.

LOCKETEER: This question is no more exciting or important than a lot of others. It is a problem that has been resolved to everyone's satisfaction. As long as I am around, there won't be any disorder.

FIFTY: And when you're no longer around?

LOCKETEER: Then someone else will be sworn into office to uphold the Sacred Law.

FIFTY: I interrupted you before. You were saying that everyone observes the terms of his contract.

LOCKETEER: Yes, everyone. And everyone knows why. People have come to realize that *fifty* years you can be sure of are far more valuable than an undetermined number of years without any kind of certainty.

FIFTY: How do you know my name? You've just mentioned my name.

LOCKETEER: I have an instinct for names. I've learned a few things in this job.

FIFTY: Can you always tell people's ages just by looking at them?

LOCKETEER: In most cases. And if I'm not absolutely sure, I'm not saying anything.

FIFTY: Then why do you need the lockets? When you're called to a dead person, one look will do for you to know his age.

LOCKETEER: That is correct. But the rite I had been sworn in to calls for another procedure.

FIFTY: Has it ever happened that someone lost his locket?

LOCKETEER: You're asking too many questions. Do you insist on an answer?

FIFTY: Yes. I want to know.

LOCKETEER: It has happened.

FIFTY: That is terrible.

LOCKETEER: Does it surprise you that we too have our share of criminals?

FIFTY: Criminals?

LOCKETEER: Criminals! Trying to eradicate all traces of his contract is the worst crime anyone could commit. He is alive only because of his contract. Without his contract he'd be nothing. Anyone trying to do away with his locket wants to steal more years than are due to him. As if that would do him any good!

FIFTY: But he could've lost it! During a swim or in a fire.

LOCKETEER: That's highly unlikely. Because everyone knows that he mustn't be without his locket, and if it is lost or broken, he has the fatal obligation to report it to me. Anyone failing to do so, places himself outside society. He *wants* to live only without the locket and he is a *murderer*.

FIFTY: So that's what a murderer is! I always had a different notion of what a murderer is.

LOCKETEER: Your notion belongs to history. Today nobody can kill another person unless he attacks him in his *moment*. But even if he'd stab him to death, he wouldn't really be guilty of his death because at that moment the other one would have died anyway.

FIFTY: How strange. But why are people without lockets called murderers?

LOCKETEER: That only becomes clear when the historical process is understood. In the initial phase of this landmark institution, it happened that violent individuals from the lower strata of our population attacked others to steal their lockets. At that time there were still a few who'd drop dead from the shock. Consequently, violent acts against the locket had the stigma of murder attached to it. In the course of time the same expression was used for those who violated their own lockets.

FIFTY: It really seems to be the most sacred thing on earth.

LOCKETEER: There is nothing more sacred. Isn't that clear to you yet?

FIFTY: It's beginning to become clear to me. But now, what really happens if you come across someone who has just passed away and he is *without* his locket.

LOCKETEER: Try to answer this question yourself.

FIFTY: You *guess* the dead person's age. You make do without the locket. You don't say that you found nothing and you file in the register whatever your trained eye has come up with.

LOCKETEER: Do you think that this is wrong?

FIFTY: How can I tell? But it seems that I guessed right. (*The Locketeer is silent.*) Now what if you happen to be wrong in a case like that? You are called to someone who has just passed away. You're looking for the locket. Your hand is well trained, I am sure—it works as if you had to find a treasure on a corpse, in the old days that would have been called a desecration, but we're living in an advanced culture—so you quickly search these so-called remains of a human being, and soon, possibly within thirty seconds, you know that there's no locket. You're stunned, because this kind of thing doesn't happen to you often, I'm sure.

LOCKETEER: It happens very rarely, thank God.

FIFTY: But your reaction may interfere with your judgment. It could happen that some day you'll really have a shock. You come to a highly respected man, a man who had received the highest honors for his accomplishments in the service of his fellow men, and suddenly, in the presence of all his relatives, friends and admirers, you discover that this great, much revered and well-known man was a murderer. That could be a very frightening experience. That could be a shock even to an authority of your rank and experience.

LOCKETEER: Why should I deny it? It never fails to shock me.

FIFTY: It must be a great shock to you. You're in a state of panic. Because at that moment everything depends on your judgment. Your eyes may be tired. You might be sick.

LOCKETEER: And even if this were the case—what's the conclusion?

FIFTY: You might be guessing the wrong age. You might, in this case at least, never find out for sure whether the man died at the right time. His contract, for once, might not coincide with himself.

LOCKETEER: The contract is always correct. *I* might make a mistake. My office is a lofty and venerable institution, but I am not a god. I can make mistakes. The contract never makes mistakes.

FIFTY: But that's not what I want to know. You are obligated to believe in the validity of the contract. But you cannot say for sure that its accuracy is proven in every single case.

LOCKETEER: No, I can't. But that's unnecessary.

FIFTY: Nothing is unnecessary. Because if one could prove that mistakes in the contracts have happened, it might also happen that someone lives longer than his name says.

LOCKETEER: I refuse to listen to you any longer. You're well on your way to becoming a murderer. Your locket is itching on your bare chest. Soon it's going to burn you up. You're not the first one who has talked to me like that. You won't be the first one to end up a common murderer. I warn you! It would be a pity. It really is a shame.

FIFTY: My locket doesn't burn me up. You'll find it right on my chest. I know that your civilian name is One-hundred-twenty-two. Don't worry. You'll find my locket where it belongs. It's my name that burns me up. Every name burns me up. Death burns me up.

GRANDMOTHER AND GRANDDAUGHTER

GRANDDAUGHTER: And where did people go then, Grandma?

GRANDMOTHER: They boarded a ship, but the ship was very crowded. The captain said: "I have too many passengers." But the people were so desperate, they all wanted to get out of this dangerous place and the captain felt very sorry for them. He had a good heart and he thought of his own children back home. So he let them all board the ship and as soon as the people of the other villages saw how kind the captain was, they all came running to him and they begged and they cried and the captain gave in and let them all on the ship. But now there really were too many of them and when the ship reached high waters they got scared. A storm was coming up, the clouds were dark and the people were thrown back and forth. The captain saw that they would be lost if nothing was done to lighten the ship. He exclaimed in his powerful voice: "We are lost! Two dozen passengers have to leave the ship. Volunteers please step forward! Who will sacrifice himself for the others?" But that wasn't easy. The waves were high and no one wanted to jump in the water.

GRANDDAUGHTER: It was too wet for them, Grandma, wasn't it? It was too wet.

GRANDMOTHER: It was also dangerous. It meant certain death.

GRANDDAUGHTER: What does that mean, Grandma, certain death?

GRANDMOTHER: That was in the old, old times. Back then, if something dangerous happened, people died right away.

GRANDDAUGHTER: Right away?

GRANDMOTHER: Yes, right away.

GRANDDAUGHTER: Then was that the *moment*, Grandma?

GRANDMOTHER: No, it wasn't. That's the whole point. Back then it could happen any time. A little girl would walk in the street, hit her head and dead she was.

GRANDDAUGHTER: She might just have hurt herself. I hurt myself sometimes.

GRANDMOTHER: Yes, but you'll always be all right again. Back then, you'd never know if you'd be all right again. Back then, it could've hurt so much that the little girl had to die.

GRANDDAUGHTER: But I could never hurt myself that much, right, Grandma?

GRANDMOTHER: No, you couldn't.

GRANDDAUGHTER: And if I get run over?

GRANDMOTHER: You might lose a leg.

GRANDDAUGHTER: Then I'd only have one leg?

GRANDMOTHER: Then you'd only have one leg and you'd get a second one made of wood so that later on nobody would notice.

GRANDDAUGHTER: And then I'd live happily ever after?

GRANDMOTHER: Not ever after. But until your *moment*.

GRANDDAUGHTER: When is my *moment*, Grandma?

GRANDMOTHER: You know it. I've told you many times.

GRANDDAUGHTER: I forgot.

GRANDMOTHER: You didn't forget.

GRANDDAUGHTER: Yes, I did!

GRANDMOTHER: You're only saying that because you want to hear me tell you again, you little cheat!

GRANDDAUGHTER: Grandma! I'm not a cheat! But if I admit that I am will you tell me my *moment*?

GRANDMOTHER: Why don't you tell me instead?

GRANDDAUGHTER: I can't count.

GRANDMOTHER: You'll have to learn it.

GRANDDAUGHTER: Will you help me?

GRANDMOTHER: I'd love to help you. But you also have to help.

GRANDDAUGHTER: I will. We'll figure it out together.

GRANDMOTHER: How about the people on the ship? Don't you want to know what happened to them?

GRANDDAUGHTER: Oh, they're stupid, you know.

GRANDMOTHER: Stupid? Why stupid?

GRANDDAUGHTER: They don't know anything. They don't even dare to jump in the water. They're afraid of the water. I'd jump right away.

GRANDMOTHER: But you know that nothing would happen to you.

GRANDDAUGHTER: They were stupid, back then. It's just a fairy tale, that's all.

GRANDMOTHER: But you like fairy tales.

GRANDDAUGHTER: When they're about smart people. Could the captain have jumped in the water?

GRANDMOTHER: He could have.

GRANDDAUGHTER: Would anything have happened to him?

GRANDMOTHER: Yes, of course. He would have died. Everybody would have died. That's how it was back then. If nobody came to save them, they died.

GRANDDAUGHTER: There, you see! Even the captain! Those were stupid times.

GRANDMOTHER: You rather live now, wouldn't you!

GRANDDAUGHTER: I much much rather live now, Grandma. Now there are no giants and no cannibals and people don't always die. You know your *moment,* don't you, Grandma?

GRANDMOTHER: Of course I know. Everybody knows his *moment.*

GRANDDAUGHTER: Will you tell me? Tell me! Tell me! Please, Grandma, tell me! I want to know, tell me! I'll be such a good girl! I'll always do my homework. I'll always do what you say! I'll never eat candy again if you say so! I'll never lie again! Please! Pretty please! Will you tell me!

GRANDMOTHER: The ideas you have, silly goose! Nobody would ever tell! Just imagine, if everyone would know! You'd make a public spectacle of yourself!

GRANDDAUGHTER: But why, Grandma? I know mine.

GRANDMOTHER: But everyone keeps that nicely to himself. No one talks about it. It's a secret. A child might tattle, but then it's only a child. Big people never tell. You just don't do that. It would be so embarrassing!

GRANDDAUGHTER: Grandma, if I won't tell anyone—does that mean that I'm a big girl?

GRANDMOTHER: If you never ever talk about it again, if you keep it all to yourself forever and ever, then you are a big girl.

GRANDDAUGHTER: And if I talk about it to you?

GRANDMOTHER: If it's too hard for you to keep it all to yourself then it's better you talk to me. But one day you'll be so big that you don't have to talk about it to anyone anymore. Then you'll really be a big girl.

GRANDDAUGHTER: To no one at all? No one in the whole wide world?

GRANDMOTHER: To no one in the whole wide world.

GRANDDAUGHTER: Not even to my doll?

GRANDMOTHER: Not even to your doll.

GRANDDAUGHTER: Grandma, I'm starting today. I know exactly when my moment will be. Do you believe me?

GRANDMOTHER: Of course I believe you!

GRANDDAUGHTER: I don't have to figure it out, not even with you. Now I'm a big girl, aren't I? Now I'm really big!

GRANDMOTHER: Yes, now you are.

FIFTY AND BOY

(*Fifty crosses the street, a stone is hurled at his head. Another one follows, then a third and a fourth.*)

FIFTY: Who's throwing rocks? Who's throwing rocks here? Hey! What's that all about? Stop it, will you! You just wait till I catch you! I'll get you! I'll find you. Stop it, I said, stop it! What a crazy thing to do! (*He notices a boy behind a pillar.*) It's you? Where are all the others? What on earth do you think you're doing?

BOY: I didn't do it.

FIFTY: What've you got in your hand?

BOY: (*Quickly drops a few stones.*) Nothing.

FIFTY: There! You just dropped a few stones!

BOY: I didn't throw any.

FIFTY: Who else did? Where are the others?

BOY: There are no others.

FIFTY: You've got no friends?

BOY: No. I'm all alone.

FIFTY: Then you threw those rocks.

BOY: I didn't.

FIFTY: And you're lying on top of it. If you have to throw rocks you could at least have the courage to admit it. Otherwise you're a coward.

BOY: I'm not a coward.

FIFTY: Then admit that you threw those rocks.

BOY: I did.

FIFTY: That's better. And why did you throw them?

BOY: Because I can.

FIFTY: What's that supposed to mean? Why should you be allowed to throw rocks?

BOY: *I* can. I can do anything I want.

FIFTY: Who gave you permission?

BOY: My mother.

FIFTY: And I'm supposed to believe that? You're lying again.

BOY: I'm not lying. I'm not a coward.

FIFTY: Then let me ask your parents. Take me to your parents!

BOY: (*Comes out from behind the pillar, gives him his hand and says, very sincerely.*) You want to come with me? I'll take you there. It's not very far.

FIFTY: Aren't you afraid of your parents?

BOY: Oh no. I'm not afraid. I'm not afraid of anybody.

FIFTY: But you'll be punished! I'm going to tell them what you did.

BOY: You can come. You can tell them. My mother won't do anything to me. My father won't either.

FIFTY: You're a strange boy.

BOY: Why am I strange?

FIFTY: What does your teacher say when you throw rocks?

BOY: I don't have a teacher.

FIFTY: But you must go to school and there must be a teacher there.

BOY: I don't go to school. I don't have a teacher.

FIFTY: Is that so? And you want me to believe that! A boy your age must go to some kind of school.

BOY: But I don't.

FIFTY: And why not? Are you sick?

BOY: Oh no, I'm not sick.

FIFTY: I wouldn't have thought so. The way you're throwing rocks you seem pretty healthy to me.

BOY: I'm never sick.

FIFTY: Then why don't you go to school?

BOY: Because I don't want to.

FIFTY: Don't your parents want you to go to school?

BOY: Oh no.

FIFTY: Do you know how to read and write?

BOY: No. I don't like to.

FIFTY: Don't your parents want you to learn how to read and write?

BOY: I don't like to. I don't want to.

FIFTY: And what are you going to do when you grow up? (*Boy is silent.*) Have you thought about it? All the other boys will be reading books and they'll laugh about you. (*Boy is silent.*) You don't mind when everybody's laughing at you?

BOY: Nobody's laughing about me.

FIFTY: But when you're bigger! Then everybody's going to think you're stupid!

BOY: I'm not stupid!

FIFTY: That's what you'll have to prove. That's why boys like you go to school.

BOY: I don't have to go.

FIFTY: Is there anything you have to do?

BOY: Not me.

FIFTY: But you always can throw rocks instead. So you stand around the street all day and throw rocks.

BOY: I can do anything I want.

FIFTY: You're the strangest boy I've ever met. What's your name?

BOY: My name is Ten.

TWO COLLEAGUES

COLLEAGUE ONE: I can't finish it.

COLLEAGUE TWO: You're not trying hard enough.

ONE: But I'm working so hard. I try everything. I'm working all day and half the night. I hardly eat. I hardly sleep. Can't you tell from the way I look that I'm overdoing it?

TWO: You're right. Now that I look at you more closely, I have to agree with you. You're working much too hard.

ONE: And still, I'm telling you, I won't be able to finish.

TWO: How can that be? Perhaps your standards are too high.

ONE: I won't make it. I won't be able to finish.

TWO: But that's entirely up to you!

ONE: That's easy to say.

TWO: Is there too much noise? Are there too many disruptions? Do you need more peace and quiet to concentrate?

ONE: It is perfectly quiet. I couldn't wish for better working conditions.

TWO: Then what are you complaining about?

ONE: I don't have enough time?

TWO: But why?

ONE: Have you ever wondered how old I might be?

TWO: No, I never do that. I hate indiscretions. I never lose any sleep over the true age of my friends. It's a secret and it will remain a secret. I have too much respect for a person's *integrity* to start digging in such private matters. To me, a human being is something *untouchable*.

ONE: But you do know my name.

TWO: Of course I do. Everyone knows. I can't shut my ears to what is public knowledge. I know at what age you're going to die; but I don't know your present age. That's a secret. I think it's very good that everyone has this secret he keeps to himself. It gives you the freedom to organize your life exactly the way you want to.

ONE: You really think so?

TWO: Yes. Nobody can tell you what to do with yourself. Because nobody knows how many years you still have to live. But you know and you can live accordingly. You are born with a certain capital of years. It won't decrease, it won't increase. Nobody can take it away from you. It is inalienably written in your name. You can't throw it out because you receive it in yearly installments. You're the only one who knows how much you have; so no one can tell you what to do. It all depends on you reaching for your own sky. If you know how to plan, you'll be able to get something out of life. You simply have to know what to buy with your time. You're the only one to blame if you don't make the best of it.

ONE: But you may have great things in mind and then simply not have the time to achieve them.

TWO: Then you overestimated yourself, that's all. That's your own fault. Why don't you have a better sense of the scope of your projects.

ONE: You can't plan everything ahead. Some projects may grow in time.

TWO: Then you will have to revise and limit them.

ONE: I can't do that. They've become too much a part of myself. I have to go on the way I started out.

TWO: Then nobody can help you.

ONE: It hurts me more than I can tell you. I can see the end very clearly. I'm sure I won't be able to finish.

TWO: I'm very sorry to hear that.

ONE: Because you don't know how old I am. I've always looked younger than I was. It's so misleading. It's awful!

TWO: Oh. Really.

ONE: I'll tell you. I'll tell you how old I am. You'll be surprised.

TWO: But I don't want to know.

ONE: And if I tell you voluntarily?

TWO: I don't want to know. I've told you already how much I hate indiscretions. It's sad enough when a man has come to a point where he wants to reveal his innermost secret. But I don't like to be an accomplice. I don't participate in things like that.

ONE: It would mean a great relief to me. It might shock you a bit. But you would understand why I'm so worried. Because I *can't* finish under the circumstances. I want to tell you.

TWO: I won't permit you to give me this kind of information! Your age is of no interest to me. It wouldn't shock me either. I refuse to be shocked about things like that. It's criminal to bother other people, let alone friends, with such private matters. Keep your years to yourself.

ONE: If only it were a matter of years!

TWO: I don't believe you're doing this! I won't have it though. I won't listen to any of your hints. There are people who *lie* and try to impress their friends with fantastic confessions about their age. It's a form of bragging you don't seem to be a stranger to.

ONE: You're seeing it all wrong. I simply want to tell someone. Nobody wants to know. Everybody takes off as soon as I start talking about it. Is it that terrible to know how old someone is?

TWO: No. That fact alone might not be terrible at all. It's the reason, the reason that forces you to tell it, that's what's so terrible. You want to complain that you have to die soon. You want to spread bad feelings among people. You want everybody to feel as miserable as you do.

ONE: How can you say that? I am only thinking about my work!

TWO: You don't believe that yourself! I know those tricks. You walk around in search of a victim. You're too weak to quietly bear what everyone else has to bear all by himself. You are a coward. You are despicable. You are afraid of your *moment.* You are a freak!

ONE: A coward. Despicable. A freak. I am afraid of my *moment.*

THE COUPLE

SHE: So brief!

HE: But we'll see each other again.

SHE: Will we?

HE: Yes. We are in love.

SHE: But will we see each other again?

HE: Weren't you happy?

HSE: Happy—oh so happy!

HE: Then you'll come again.

SHE: I don't know.

HE: You're hurting me. How can you hurt me so?

SHE: I don't mean to hurt you. I love you very much.

HE: Then tell me when you'll come again.

SHE: I don't know.

HE: You've got to know.

SHE: Don't torture me. I can't tell.

HE: Why? What's holding you back?

SHE: Don't ask so many questions.

HE: But I can't live without knowing when you'll be back again. I want to know. I won't let you go if you don't tell me. I'll lock you up. I won't let you get out. I'll keep you prisoner.

SHE: That won't do much good.

HE: You won't let me lock you up?

SHE: No.

HE: But it's been so beautiful up to a minute ago. You came to me. I've never loved anyone as much as you.

SHE: That's what one says. That's what one thinks.

HE: I don't just say so. I don't just think so. I know it. I can't live without you.

SHE: You'll have to try.

HE: I know I won't be able to.

SHE: You'd be surprised about the things one is able to do.

HE: It might help if I knew why you won't be coming back.

SHE: Are you sure that would make it easier for you?

HE: Yes. It'll never be easy. It breaks my heart. But there might be a reason which you can't help. Something beyond your control.

SHE: That is it. It's beyond my control. I can't see you again.

HE: But maybe that's only what you think. Maybe I can do something. I'll do anything to see you again. Anything. Just tell me! Tell me!

SHE: There's nothing you can do.

HE: That's impossible. We only have to want something and we can do it! There is nothing we can not do! Nothing!

SHE: That's a child's fantasy.

HE: You came today, didn't you? You made it possible. Why not tomorrow!

Why not tomorrow!

SHE: It's not possible tomorrow.

HE: Then the day after tomorrow! I'll be thinking about you all day tomorrow, as long as I can see you the day after. I'll stay awake until then. I won't go to sleep for two nights. I'll be seeing you in front of me. Not for one moment will I let go of your image as long as I know you'll be here again.

SHE: *Moment.*

HE: (*Startles.*) *Moment*? Why did you say that? What do you mean?

SHE: I didn't say anything.

HE: Yes, you did! You did! You said a horrible thing.

SHE: What did I say?

HE: *Moment.*

SHE: That's what I thought. Did I say it?

HE: Yes. What did you mean?

SHE: I didn't mean to frighten you.

HE: Nothing can frighten me. Tell me! Just tell me!

SHE: Tomorrow is my birthday.

HE: Your birthday.

SHE: My last birthday—you understand.

HE: Your last birthday. How could you do that?

SHE: That's why I came. That's why I came to you.

FIFTY AND A YOUNG WOMAN AT THE FUNERAL OF HER CHILD

FIFTY: Young lady! Young lady! I must talk to you. Don't get scared, young lady. I don't know who you are. I don't even know your name. But I do know that this is the funeral of your child. Please, tell me, young lady, I implore you! Talk to me! Tell me—did you lose your child?

YOUNG WOMAN: Yes.

FIFTY: He was very young?

YOUNG WOMAN: Yes.

FIFTY: How old was he?

YOUNG WOMAN: Seven.

FIFTY: You are heart-broken.

YOUNG WOMAN: No.

FIFTY: You loved him very much?

YOUNG WOMAN: Yes.

FIFTY: And you aren't upset?

YOUNG WOMAN: No. Not at all.

FIFTY: Why not?

YOUNG WOMAN: I knew that he had to die. I always knew.

FIFTY: You must've been very upset while he was still alive.

YOUNG WOMAN: No, I wasn't.

FIFTY: Didn't you feel sorry for him that he had to die so young?

YOUNG WOMAN: I knew it when he was born.

FIFTY: Would you have liked to have done something about it?

YOUNG WOMAN: That was impossible to do.

FIFTY: Did you try?

YOUNG WOMAN: No. No one would do such a thing.

FIFTY: But if you'd have been the first one to try?

YOUNG WOMAN: Me? The only one? Never!

FIFTY: You'd never do anything if you were the only one?

YOUNG WOMAN: I would've been so ashamed.

FIFTY: Ashamed? Why?

YOUNG WOMAN: They would have ostracized me. They would have said: Something's wrong with her.

FIFTY: But if you could have saved him? If you could've kept him alive for one more year?

YOUNG WOMAN: (*Aghast.*) That's theft! That is a crime!

FIFTY: Why is it a crime?

YOUNG WOMAN: That is blasphemy!

FIFTY: Why is it blasphemy?

YOUNG WOMAN: His time is predetermined. *One year!*

FIFTY: Could you imagine what this year would've been like?

YOUNG WOMAN: (*Still aghast.*) I would've been afraid all the time. I would have felt very strange about my own child. I would have felt as if I had stolen my own child. I've never stolen a thing in my life. I would never steal anything. I am an honest woman. I would've had to keep him hidden. I would've had it written all over me that I was keeping something stolen in my house.

FIFTY: But he was your child! How can you steal your own child?

YOUNG WOMAN: I would have stolen that one year. He wasn't entitled to it. He was only seven! How could I burden him with such a theft!

FIFTY: What if it would've been only one month?

YOUNG WOMAN: I can't imagine it. The more I think about it the more horrifying you seem to me.

FIFTY: What about one day? One single day! If you could have had him alive for one more day. Just a day. One day is so short!

YOUNG WOMAN: You frighten me! You are evil! You are trying to tempt me. But I won't give in to you! *One day!* One whole day! Every minute I'd have only been thinking: Now they're coming to get me. I always looked after my child. I gave him plenty to eat. I dressed him well. He was the nicest-looking kid on the block. He was popular. Everybody loved him. He never caused any trouble. Everybody will tell you that. Ask the people who were at the funeral! Ask the neighbors! Go ahead, talk to the neighbors if you don't believe me. I've done everything a mother's supposed to do. I was very conscientious. I was up many nights when he was calling for me. I never said an angry word to him. I loved him. Everyone will tell you that.

FIFTY: I believe it. I believe it.

TWO YOUNG GENTLEMEN

FIRST YOUNG GENTLEMAN: What are we going to do today?

SECOND YOUNG GENTLEMAN: What are we going to do today! Same as we always do, I'd say.

FIRST: Which is?

SECOND: Take a guess.

FIRST: What do you think?

SECOND: Nothing.

FIRST: That's right. Nothing. It's always nothing.

SECOND: It's always been nothing.

FIRST: And it always will be nothing.

SECOND: That's life.

FIRST: *What* a bore! *What* a bore!

SECOND: But it's always been that way.

FIRST: It couldn't have been that boring in the old days.

SECOND: Why not?

FIRST: Because nobody would've been able to take it.

SECOND: What could have been so different then? They were always human beings, always up to the same old stupidities, always driven by the same petty appetites, which sometimes came in grandiose disguises.

FIRST: It certainly was completely different then. Can you imagine what it means to *kill* someone?

SECOND: No. I can't. We've left that sort of barbarian nonsense far behind.

FIRST: You call it nonsense! I'd give anything to be able to kill someone.

SECOND: What's holding you back?

FIRST: What's holding me back? Everything! I know too much. I know that it isn't up to me whether the person I attack is going to die or not. If I do it at the wrong moment, he won't die. Whatever I do, it's not my doing. Even the lowest person is safe from me.

SECOND: That is true. But that is exactly what we are so proud of.

FIRST: Proud! But I long for the times when you could *confront* your enemy and actually *get rid* of him! Can you imagine: a *duel*!

SECOND: Yes, that must've been great.

FIRST: You never knew what would happen. You could never be sure. It might be you, it might be the other.

SECOND: Sometimes it was neither.

FIRST: All the better. Then you could go challenge someone else.

SECOND: Until one day it had to happen.

FIRST: And if it happened to be your bullet that hit the mark, you knew it was you who killed him, all by yourself, no one interfered, it was a clear case: you have killed the man.

SECOND: But then what? Then you had to hide or flee. Then you were a murderer.

FIRST: All right. Why not? I wouldn't mind being that kind of a murderer. At
least I'd know why they call me that.

SECOND: Not like today.

FIRST: Today? What's a murderer today? An ordinary locket thief! That's
what they call a murderer! His victim is alive and well, still he deserves to
be called a murderer! Big deal! You know, I think that's really an outrage.
If you can't kill anyone then don't mess with the word for it either.

SECOND: I've thought so too, sometimes. But, that's the way it is.

FIRST: And there's nothing you can do about it. That's what's so awful. They
really got you in a bind. Since you're no longer able to kill anyone you're
no longer able to change anything.

SECOND: You are right! I've never thought about it that way.

FIRST: Things will stay forever the way they are.

SECOND: Forever. And you'll never be able to kill anyone.

FIRST: Never. What a shame!

TWO LADIES

FIRST LADY: What would you say? You've got a good eye.

SECOND LADY: I'd say, just about a year. Maybe less.

FIRST: You think she's still got one year?

SECOND: Maybe less. Maybe only half a year.

FIRST: She keps hinting that she's got more. Sometimes she tells me six, sometimes she tells me seven.

SECOND: Terrific! She wants it to get around.

FIRST: She keeps whispering it in my ear and implores me not to tell anyone.

SECOND: She's counting on your indiscretion.

FIRST: Do you know that she is still hoping for a husband?

SECOND: What? With her one year? Who is she kidding? No man would go
near her. With one year! No man would take her. And if she were the
greatest beauty, there isn't a man who would take her with one year. If you
were a man would you take a wife who's got just one more year?

FIRST: You want to know something? Some men would like that.

SECOND: I know all about those short-termers! No woman with any sense of
pride would get involved with that kind of man. To me, short-termers are
criminals.

FIRST: You know, some of them are very charming. I have a cousin who just
remarried and again it is a low woman. He says, it's a silly prejudice. He'd
never marry any other kind of woman. And when this one dies he's going
to take a low woman again. A low woman tries harder to leave behind a
good memory. A low woman wants to have a nice life, because she has no
time to wait. A low woman, he says, is always in a secret panic. She knows

that she can't get any further and is happy with what she has. A low woman makes fewer demands.

SECOND: Come on now, that is nonsense. A low woman wants to enjoy life because she doesn't know any better. She wants to go out every night. She wants nothing but to amuse herself. She always wants new lovers and new clothes. She just takes and takes; why should she care about what happens after?

FIRST: That's what I used to think. But my cousin says that I was wrong. This is his fourth marriage to a low woman. His motto is: Hands off high women! Just imagine, he says, it's a bad marriage and you have a high wife. Whether the man can stand it or not, she'll be able to make demands until God knows what age.

SECOND: If he is happy with a low woman, and it will be over soon, it's his loss and he will have to look for a new one. I agree, there are a few decent low women here and there, but that makes it all the worse for the man who gets one of them. He won't find another one like her, believe me.

FIRST: He says if you know what you're doing, nothing can go wrong. He is very careful about whom he chooses. He has already picked the next one. And she, by the way, is even lower, he says. He hasn't quite decided about the next one after her, but he does have someone in mind.

SECOND: He's already figuring this out while the others are still alive?

FIRST: Yes, of course. That's the great advantage. He is choosing them very carefully. He asks himself, how long do I want to live with the next one, and once he is clear about that he can go ahead and look around.

SECOND: But for God's sake, are these women just sitting around waiting for him?

FIRST: Of course. Once he gets engaged to them! He is tremendously popular. Every woman would be glad to wait for him for a dozen years. But it never takes that long. He has a wonderful life. He is determined to go through two dozen marriages.

SECOND: I think that's overdoing it a bit. Anyway, how does he know how old his brides are?

FIRST: He has a very good eye for it, you know. Of course, that's because he has so much experience. It's like a sport to him, guessing the right age. He is so much in demand that some women even *tell* him their age, voluntarily.

SECOND: No man would get me to do that. These must be very shameless women!

FIRST: Well, you just were never crazy enough.

SECOND: And no one ever lies to him?

FIRST: It does happen. Some make themselves older, out of jealousy.

SECOND: Jealousy?

FIRST: Yes, there was one woman who let him know that she had two more years to go and with that understanding he married her. And believe me, she was terribly in love with him. It's always that way. They had agreed during their marriage he would look for her successor. The thought was unbearable to her but she had to agree to it, otherwise he would never have married her. So he, the way he always does it, started to take a good and careful look around and sure enough, he finds a woman, whom he found suitable. She accepted his proposal, considered herself engaged and waited—not very patiently, that is. Finally, his wife's last birthday has come. He assumes, ever so tactfully, ever so courteously—he is not a monster, I want you to know—that she is going to die. He waits all day, he waits up until late at night—nothing happens. He goes to bed thinking that when he'll wake up the next morning it's going to be all over and his wife won't get up anymore. But the next morning he opens his eyes and sees his wife, pacing the room, shaking her head, absorbed in thoughts. "What is this about?" he wants to know. "I made a mistake," she says, "I am younger than I thought I was. It's next year." He could do nothing. He knew that she had lied to him. But she stayed with him for another year much to the annoyance of her successor who felt cheated. It was a funny story. Everybody was talking about it. I'm sure you have heard about it too.

SECOND: I grant you that all this might be possible. His life might be quite entertaining. But I'd never call this love. True love is only possible with high women, no matter what you say. True love takes time. You have to get to know each other, you must go through a lot together and have blind faith in each other. Fifty years of marriage, that's my ideal.

FIRST: So you are also against low men?

SECOND: Of course I am. I am against everything low. I've always aimed for the highest.

FIRST: I can't understand how you can get through life with such high expectations.

SECOND: I've always had them. Only the best is good enough for me. A man whose name isn't Eighty-eight at the very least is of no interest to me.

FIRST: Well, yes, on the whole, you're right. But one has to learn to compromise. I used to be like you. But then, what did I finally do?

SECOND: You married an average gentleman.

FIRST: I'm also just about average.

SECOND: The average, that's what I always hated the most. I even think you would have done better marrying a very low person, say a Twenty or a Thirty, and to go for the high life afterwards.

FIRST: I'm a creature of habit. I get used to a man and then I don't want anybody else. I'm not a romantic.

SECOND: I've noticed. Well, you're an average person, that's all.

FIRST: You're not all that high yourself, you know!

SECOND: I'm quite happy with my name. After all, I'm fifteen years better than you.

FIRST: You don't have to rub it in all the time.

SECOND: I don't mean to hurt you. But you must understand that we think differently about a lot of things. We were born different, that's all. I am high, you are average. Nothing we can do about that.

FIFTY IS PUBLICLY EXPOSED AT A GATHERING OF THE PEOPLE

(*The Locketeer, in heavy official attire, stands next to him. He speaks very loudly, so that everyone can hear.*)

FIFTY: This isn't my *moment*!

LOCKETEER: You are wrong! Your *moment* has come.

FIFTY: It hasn't come. I know how old I am.

LOCKETEER: Your memory is deceiving you.

FIFTY: Test my memory. Go ahead, test it! You'll see that it is right.

LOCKETEER: It is not up to me to test your memory. Perhaps you still have it, nonetheless, your *moment* is here.

FIFTY: How can my *moment* be here when my memory is correct and I know my age.

LOCKETEER: You have been misinformed. Sometimes children are being misled. There are mothers who do not obey the law. Fortunately, they are just a few.

FIFTY: But how do you know that? How did you find out that my mother has misled me?

LOCKETEER: I know it.

FIFTY: Did she tell you? You don't know her. She is still living. You only know the dead.

LOCKETEER: This is blasphemy. It is time you stop blaspheming.

THE PEOPLE: Blasphemer! Blasphemer!

FIFTY: (*To the people.*) But *I* request that you delay the execution for one day! You know it has to come. You are so sure. I am asking for one day! I am ready to confess if you grant me one more day.

LOCKETEER: The law doesn't permit any delay. But it is better for you to confess.

FIFTY: I confess that today I am fifty years old. It is true that I never bothered to think about it. I didn't admit my age, because I simply never gave a hoot. I have never believed in my *moment*.

LOCKETEER: Blasphemy again! You are defying the law!

THE PEOPLE: Do not lead us into temptation! Do not lead us into temptation!

FIFTY: (*To the people.*) I have confessed. Grant me *one* day! I am willing to let the Locketeer treat me as if I were dead. You can tie me, you can shackle me. Take all food away from me. Prevent me from sleeping. Do anything you like with me, just let me live one more day! Could it be that you aren't all that sure? Could it be that you are fearful for your law? If this is the true law, let's test it!

LOCKETEER: The law is not to be tested. The law is sacred.

FIFTY: (*Still to the people.*) This is your one chance, your last chance. Here you have a man, who never believed in his *moment*. When will you have such a rare creature in your midst again? I am not bragging about it. I am nothing special. It's a passion, just like you have your passions. It is my passion to mistrust the *moment*. We all have different passions. This happens to be mine. But this one might be useful to you. It offers the opportunity to test whether one has to die at his *moment, even if he doesn't believe in it.* I don't believe in it! Can you understand that? I don't believe in it.

LOCKETEER: This is a travesty! The man is not demented. He is a travesty, just as he tried to make a travesty out of the funeral. His mind is perfectly clear. He has talked to me like that before. I have warned him. *I* knew how it would end.

FIFTY: (*To the Locketeer.*) If you are so sure, grant me one day. You have the power. Get the people to grant me one day.

LOCKETEER: I have no power over any day. I have no power over anything.

FIFTY: That's what you say. But you know better.

LOCKETEER: Repent, before you die! You still have time. Repent!

FIFTY: I have nothing to repent. But I beg you for mercy. Grant me one day!

LOCKETEER: Coward! There is only one way for you to receive mercy: Recant and acknowledge the *moment*!

FIFTY: Oh, if I could! If only I could! I'd do it for you, because I feel sorry for you.

LOCKETEER: You have just taken the first step in the right direction. These were the first words I liked hearing from you. These were your first *human* words.

FIFTY: I'll try to find more such words for you. Will you grant me mercy if I amend?

LOCKETEER: I shall try. But don't count on my power. I don't have any.

FIFTY: But you'll try. Tell me, what will happen to me if I recant?

LOCKETEER: If you recant, you'll die naturally at your *moment*.

FIFTY: And you'll just leave me alone and let me die?

LOCKETEER: I shall try. But you don't have much time.

FIFTY: What do I have to do?

LOCKETEER: You must publicly recant.

FIFTY: In what words?

LOCKETEER: You must repeat loudly after me: I believe in the Sacred Law. Speak up, go ahead!

FIFTY: I believe in the Sacred Law.

LOCKETEER: I believe in the *moment*.

FIFTY: I believe in the *moment*.

LOCKETEER: I shall die as I was predetermined to . . .

FIFTY: I shall die as I was predetermined to . . .

LOCKETEER: And as everybody dies.

FIFTY: And as everybody dies.

LOCKETEER: Everybody has his *moment* . . .

FIFTY: Everybody has his *moment* . . .

LOCKETEER: And everybody knows his *moment*.

FIFTY: And everybody knows his *moment*.

LOCKETEER: No one ever lived beyond his *moment*.

FIFTY: No one ever lived beyond his *moment*.

LOCKETEER: I thank you for your clemency. I was blinded.

FIFTY: I thank you for your clemency. I was blinded.

LOCKETEER: You may go now.

FIFTY: Am I free to go my own way?

LOCKETEER: You are. But you are no longer the same.

FIFTY: Oh hour, sweet hour which I have gained.

LOCKETEER: Don't forget that I shall see you soon again.

FIFTY: I'll be seeing you soon again?

LOCKETEER: You won't see me. I shall be seeing you.

FIFTY: When you come to look for my locket.

LOCKETEER: Be quiet!

THE NEXT SCENE BETWEEN THE CHORUS OF THE UNEQUAL AND THE LOCKETEER FOLLOWS IMMEDIATELY

CHORUS OF THE UNEQUAL: We are grateful.

LOCKETEER: (*Chanting like a priest.*) What are you grateful for?

CHORUS: We are grateful. We have no fear.

LOCKETEER: Why do you have no fear?

CHORUS: We have no fear, because we know what lies ahead of us.

LOCKETEER: Is what lies ahead of you so wonderful?

CHORUS: It isn't wonderful. But we have no fear.

LOCKETEER: Why do you have no fear if what lies ahead of you is not wonderful? Why have you no fear?

CHORUS: We know when. We know when.

LOCKETEER: Since when do you know when?

CHORUS: Since we knew how to think.

LOCKETEER: Is it so wonderful to know when?

CHORUS: It is wonderful to know when!

LOCKETEER: Do you like to be together?

CHORUS: No, we don't like to be together.

LOCKETEER: Why are you together if you don't like to be?

CHORUS: We only seem to be together, we shall separate.

LOCKETEER: What are you waiting for?

CHORUS: We are waiting for the *moment* which will separate us.

LOCKETEER: Do you know the *moment*?

CHORUS: Everyone knows it. Everyone knows the *moment* when he will be leaving everyone else.

LOCKETEER: Do you have faith in your knowledge?

CHORUS: We do!

LOCKETEER: Are you happy? What else do you want?

CHORUS: We don't want anything else. We are happy.

LOCKETEER: You are happy, because you know the *moment*.

CHORUS: We know it. Since we know the *moment*, we have no fear of anything.

LOCKETEER: All satisfied! All satisfied!

CHORUS: All satisfied! All satisfied! All satisfied!

PART II

FIFTY AND FRIEND

FRIEND: There you are. I'm glad it's you.

FIFTY: Can you explain to me why I am still alive?

FRIEND: Wasn't what happened enough of a warning to you? What more do you want to find out?

FIFTY: Have you any idea of what actually went on?

FRIEND: Who doesn't? It's the talk of the town.

FIFTY: I wish you would have been there.

FRIEND: I couldn't have helped you anyway.

FIFTY: No. But you could have seen the whole thing, from down below.

FRIEND: Aren't you your own witness?

FIFTY: I pride myself on the fact that I remained calm and cool. I concentrated on what I wanted to know, that is, the answer to *my* question. I wanted to be heard. My only concern was how to drag out the scene as long as possible.

FRIEND: And you didn't see the crowd? You didn't feel how they all stared at you? How they were ready to tear you to pieces at just one word of the Locketeer?

FIFTY: Surely, I felt threatened. I might have been more afraid than I was willing to admit. But I also was very curious. If they were to attack me now, if they really would, as you say, tear me to pieces at just one word of the Locketeer, would this then really be the right time for me to die? Or would it be three hours before that certain *moment*? Or maybe two hours? Or one?

Can one die *before* one's *moment?*

FRIEND: But you came around just in time. I am very glad.

FIFTY: Why are you glad?

FRIEND: Because I care for you. You are here. You talk to me.

FIFTY: Do I mean that much to you?

FRIEND: I thought you knew that.

FIFTY: Does one ever know?

FRIEND: Well then, let me tell you.

FIFTY: People mean a lot to you, don't they?

FRIEND: Some do.

FIFTY: Are there many?

FRIEND: No, just a few. Maybe that is why they mean so much to me.

FIFTY: How many people do you really love?

FRIEND: I am ashamed to tell you the truth.

FIFTY: Go on.

FRIEND: Don't you know that yourself?

FIFTY: I think that of all people you feel closest to your little sister, to her image, I mean. Forgive me for mentioning her.

FRIEND: I still love her. I never got over it.

FIFTY: You've never talked about her before.

FRIEND: I never was able to. You are the only one. But in all those years I've always been thinking of her. I've never told anybody.

FIFTY: Don't you have anyone else? You're still mourning for her?

FRIEND: Yes. As long as I hadn't spoken to anyone about her, I didn't care about anyone else.

FIFTY: You never could accept it. Perhaps this is what drew me to you.

FRIEND: I could never accept it. No, I couldn't.

FIFTY: I admire you for that.

FRIEND: Oh, don't say that! Do you know what that means: years and years of pain and there is nothing that could stop it. Nothing! Nothing!

FIFTY: But has that changed in any way?

FRIEND: Just recently it has changed a bit.

FIFTY: You mean, now you feel close to someone who is alive.

FRIEND: Yes.

FIFTY: Did this happen suddenly?

FRIEND: Yes.

FIFTY: So a totally new person came into your life, and I, your best friend, didn't notice.

FRIEND: It's no one new. It's someone I've known for a long time.

FIFTY: How did this happen?

FRIEND: Your curiosity is like a hungry wolf. Yet I can't resist answering you.

FIFTY: How did it happen?

FRIEND: I talked about her to somebody.

FIFTY: About your sister?

FRIEND: Yes.

FIFTY: And now you're fond of the person to whom you talked about her.

FRIEND: Yes. Almost as much as of her.

FIFTY: But then you would have to be as fond of me.

FRIEND: It is you, don't you see! It is you I talked to. Nobody else knows about it.

FIFTY: It is me. How strange.

FRIEND: You forced me to tell the truth.

FIFTY: I hope you don't regret it. But does that surprise you? Didn't I confide in you what it is that tortures and drives me? You have done the same. You have given me your pain. Aren't we basically tortured by the same thing?

FRIEND: No. I am concerned with this one person only. I don't care what happens to the others.

FIFTY: Only now you're also concerned about me. And I do care about what happens to any of you.

FRIEND: That's exactly what worries me so much. I have the feeling that something terrible might happen to you. I was shaking when you were up there, exposed to the crowd.

FIFTY: So you were there after all.

FRIEND: Yes.

FIFTY: And you didn't want to tell me.

FRIEND: No.

FIFTY: But why not?

FRIEND: I was afraid that my being there would only encourage you in your suicidal undertaking.

FIFTY: That's true. You give me courage. I am able to talk to you. If I wouldn't have talked to you I could have never started with this.

FRIEND: But now it's all finished, isn't it?

FIFTY: Do you think so? If you can explain to me what has happened, it is finished. I'm not sure you'll be able to. But I'm glad you were there, because now you will be able to tell me *exactly* what went on. I no longer trust the things I experience all alone, since they no longer concern just me alone. Do you want to help me?

FRIEND: I will always help you. That's how it is between us. Ask me whatever you want. I'll never lie to you again. I couldn't lie to you.

FIFTY: I couldn't either when I talk to you. But now . . . . can you explain to me why I am still alive?

FRIEND: I don't understand you. It was not yet your *moment*.

FIFTY: But the Locketeer announced in front of all the people that my *moment* had come. You were there. You've heard it.

FRIEND: He is entitled to one mistake.

FIFTY: He maintained that he knew for sure and I denied it. He claimed he knew better and that my mother had misled me. How does he know? How can he know?

FRIEND: He has an eye for people. Don't forget, he's had tremendous experience. He is absolutely sure of what he is saying. If he wouldn't have been so sure he wouldn't have exposed you to half the population.

FIFTY: But what for?

FRIEND: He wanted to prove to the rest how silly your doubts were. So there you stood, pig-headed beyond belief, insisting again and again that you didn't believe it. You were going to survive your *moment*. They should just let you have your way and you would demonstrate it to them. They should be looking at you as an experiment. You didn't believe it and therefore it wouldn't happen to you.

FIFTY: That's right. That's what I said.

FRIEND: But he knew that that's not possible. He knew that at your *moment* you would drop dead all on your own and he wanted it to happen in public just as he let you challenge him in public. He wanted you to contradict yourself. You may not think that this is very nice of him, and I grant you it may seem rather malicious to turn man's frailty into a public spectacle. But don't forget what you had done before. You had disrupted a funeral and put the poor mother, who had just lost her child, through the most horrifying ordeal. The outrage against you was pretty general and it is the Locketeer's duty to assure the safety of all citizens. He has to watch out that the old fears won't surface again: Everything depends on the law of the *moment*. If someone were to permit any doubts about this law, everything would begin to fall apart, the consequences would be unspeakable. People would again start cutting each other's throats and we'd be back to the old jungle. Aren't you satisfied with the outcome? He got you to retract and you're still alive. What more do you want?

FIFTY: It's just that I don't understand. You don't answer my question.

FRIEND: Perhaps I should ask *you* a few questins. It was *your* attitude, not the Locketeer's, which nobody understood.

FIFTY: Go ahead, ask, ask me!

FRIEND: When you were led up to the platform and the people started to gather you first remained silent for a long time. More and more people came. Soon the square was packed with huge crowds of people. All this time you just let the trial go on without saying a single word. To the Locketeer's accusations you just nodded your head indifferently. Then suddenly, when he had already passed the sentence, you exclaimed, "This isn't my *moment*." You sounded incredibly sure of yourself and I can't tell you how deeply you had impressed the people with those first words. The Locketeer, however, seemed to know better and he came down hard on you. You referred to your memory and to your mother. You were absolutely sure that this wasn't your *moment*. The Locketeer repeated the sentence. I admired you very much and despite my unspeakable fear for you I prayed that you should stand firm. Then all of a sudden you started to beg for one day's delay and for this one day you offered a *confession*. What you confessed was—and I still don't understand it—that *yes, it was your moment after all,* exactly the opposite of the first words which you had spoken so loud and strong. The impact of your contradiction was tremendous. Immediately, the general mood turned against you. You must know that ever since then everybody takes you for a charlatan. Can you explain this contradiction to me?

FIFTY: Nothing's easier than that. It is no contradiction. I simply don't *know*. I don't know how old I am. I never bothered to think about it. Until recently, I didn't even know that one is supposed to know that. I don't really know my birthday. Everybody always made such a big secret out of it. I am a victim of this general hush, so much so that I didn't even notice that something was always hushed over. They must have told me quite a few times when I was a child: But by then I had already learned not to hear certain things. And even if I knew it, I forgot it later on. I never wasted nor saved my years. I never looked at them as capital. I simply never thought about years. I liked life too much to bother thinking about them.

FRIEND: You really don't know how old you are?

FIFTY: No. What I said was wrong both times. I lied both times.

FRIEND: But what sense is that supposed to make?

FIFTY: I wanted to confuse the Locketeer. If I *deny* my *moment,* how *can* the Locketeer prove it? That's what I said to myself. I wanted to confuse him in front of that huge crowd. I wanted to shake up their false faith. Someone had to do it. I am the right person because I don't know my age.

FRIEND: A desperate undertaking. Their faith is not false.

FIFTY: But I succeeded. Don't you see that I succeeded?

FRIEND: You shouldn't talk like that. Don't forget that you recanted.

FIFTY: First I forced him to insist that my *moment* had come. He was absolutely sure and everybody heard him say so. Then I recanted for which he granted me mercy. I am still alive. Either he made a mistake and knows no more about my *moment* than I do or it is possible *to survive the moment itself.* From now on everybody has to believe in either of these two possibilities.

FRIEND: How wrong you are! Everybody remembers your retraction, which made a significant impression. The only thing they got out of the entire procedure was the fact that *you* contradicted yourself.

FIFTY: Maybe. It doesn't matter to me. As far as I am concerned, I've come further than I've ever been. I know now that the Locketeer *lies* at least occasionally. His estimates are by no means certain. He himself is uncertain. He defends something that is uncertain. He contradicts himself and he pardons you if you recant. He needs this *recantation,* he'd do anything for a recantation. He depends on it as we depend on lockets.

FRIEND: I must admit I also had that impression.

FIFTY: You admit it? You admit it? That was your personal impression? And you were down in the street, you were not in danger, so your judgment couldn't have been affected by nerves and excitement.

FRIEND: Don't think I was any less excited or nervous than you. But I had hoped that your recantation was *valid,* that is to say, final, that you were sick of fighting against natural laws.

FIFTY: Did you say natural laws? You mean the regulations of the Locketeer's office? As of now I don't even know what's inside a locket. If I could increase by ten the years which are allocated to any of us in writing inside the capsule—if I could open a locket and increase the number by ten—what do you think might happen?

FRIEND: You are not going to turn into a criminal. You are not going to become someone's murderer! I know you too well. You aren't a murderer. This is not how a murderer feels. This is not how a murderer talks. You'll calm down. You've been through great excitement. You'll calm down and forget everything and leave it at your recantation. Promise me!

FIFTY: I don't promise anything.

FIFTY AND TWO VERY OLD WOMEN

FIFTY: Hey, listen to me! Hey you! I want to talk to you two! Why are you running away from me? I won't hurt you! Hey, stop running! I have to talk to you!

FIRST OLD WOMAN: (*Breathless.*) We don't have anything.

SECOND OLD WOMAN: (*Breathless.*) Absolutely nothing!

FIFTY: But I don't want anything! I don't want to take anything from you. I only want to ask you something.

FIRST: I'm not from here.

SECOND: I'm from far away.

FIFTY: I don't want to ask you for directions. I know my way.

FIRST: So what is it? What?

SECOND: We don't have anything and we aren't from here.

FIFTY: You don't have to be afraid of me. Don't you understand? I won't hurt you. I promise. Cross my heart. I only want to ask you something. About the old times.

FIRST: Very old. But she's older.

SECOND: She's older. Ask her.

FIFTY: I want to ask you both.

FIRST: It's getting late.

SECOND: I've got to run.

FIFTY: How are you going to run? I'll take you home afterwards. It won't take any time at all. Now just stand still for a minute and listen to what I want to ask you.

FIRST: I'm listening. I can hear you all right. But I don't know anything.

SECOND: I hear pretty well. I'm not that old. But I don't know what to tell you.

FIFTY: Now listen carefully. I want to know something from each of you. (*To the First Old Woman.*) How old are you?

FIRST: I'm not old.

FIFTY: I know. But *how* old are you?

FIRST: I can't remember. Why don't you ask her?

FIFTY: Why don't you think about it while I'm asking her? (*To the Second Old Woman.*) How old are you?

SECOND: Who says I'm old?

FIFTY: All right. But *how* old?

SECOND: I forgot. Ask her.

FIFTY: (*To the First Old Woman.*) Do you know now? Did you remember?

FIRST: No. I know nothing. It's been far too long ago.

FIFTY: And if I beat you up, you still won't tell me?

FIRST: (*Screams.*) Help! Help! He wants to beat me up!

FIFTY: Be quiet. I won't beat you up. What's your name?

FIRST: Ninety-three, but don't beat me up! I'm telling you, Ninety-three!

SECOND: I'll tell you too. But don't hurt me. My name is Ninety-six.

FIFTY: You're telling me even before I'm asking. You must be in a big hurry. How long have you been friends?

BOTH: Forever.

FIFTY: But I want to know how long.

FIRST: I knew her even before I got married.

SECOND: Me too.

FIFTY: You must have married very young.

FIRST: Oh, much too young. No one knew how young I really was. Now they're all dead. Now she's the only one left.

SECOND: I've always been older than her. She's always been lagging behind me.

FIFTY: Now I'll soon know how old you are.

BOTH: Oh no. No one knows that.

FIFTY: I only have to look in your lockets.

BOTH: (*Start to scream.*) That's not true. He is a liar. He's lying! He's lying!

FIFTY: Stop screaming! Right now!

BOTH: (*Shrieking louder and louder.*) It's not true. No one knows. He's lying! He's lying!

FIFTY: I'm going to beat you up! If you don't stop screaming this minute, I'm going to beat you up!

FIRST: (*Shaking.*) I'll stop. I'm so scared!

SECOND: I want to stop! I can't. I'm so afraid!

FIFTY: Give me your lockets. Right now!

FIRST: I don't have a locket.

SECOND: I've lost mine. (*Both are completely calm now.*)

FIFTY: I'll find them. You both still have them. Give them to me. I need them.

FIRST: I've eaten mine.

FIFTY: (*Grabbing her.*) Then spit it out!

FIRST: (*Keeps spitting.*) Nothing's coming.

FIFTY: That's even better! Why don't you just give it to me. Otherwise I'll kill you both.

SECOND: (*Trembling.*) I found mine. Here it is. (*She hands him the locket.*) She's got hers too. Go see for yourself!

FIRST: You should be ashamed of yourself! You only want me to lose mine too!

FIFTY: Just hand it over without a fight. You see, she's given me hers.

FIRST: (*Hands him her locket, crying.*) What am I going to do without my locket?

SECOND: What's going to happen to us?

FIFTY: I'll give you different ones, much prettier ones, made of gold.

BOTH: Gold! Gold!

FIFTY: (*Puts a locket around each.*) There. Now you've got much prettier lockets. You better be happy now, huh! Now you'll go on living for a long time. Because those are good-luck lockets. I make them myself. But you mustn't tell anyone. If you don't tell anyone, you'll each be living much much longer.

FIRST: Oh yes. Much longer!

SECOND: Much much longer!

FIFTY: The next time I see you you'll get even prettier ones. I'll find you, don't worry. I know where you are. But now you must leave very quietly. You must promise me that you won't tell anyone. Otherwise everyone'll want such beautiful gold lockets and I've only got those two. If people find out about them, they'll want to take them away from you. Will you keep your mouths shut?

FIRST: Oh yes! Oh yes!

SECOND: But I'll be getting a prettier one!

FIFTY: You will. I'll have to look for it first. That's not so easy. I'll have to go away to do that. When I come back, I'll meet you again, then you'll be getting those other lockets. With the ones you have now you've got all the time in the world to wait. But now you better leave quickly before anyone notices anything. They'll steal your lockets if you don't watch out!

BOTH: (*Hobbling away in a hurry.*) Thank you kindly. Thank you kindly. Thank you!

FIFTY AND FRIEND

FIFTY: I have two lockets.

FRIEND: You have what?

FIFTY: I have two lockets. Two real lockets.

FRIEND: For God's sake, where did you get those?

FIFTY: I got them from two little old women. Now they belong to me. I can do with them whatever I want.

FRIEND: I . . . I don't want to see them.

FIFTY: That doesn't alter the fact that I have them.

FRIEND: That's terrible. Give them back immediately!

FIFTY: I gave them better ones.

FRIEND: Better ones?

FIFTY: Yes. Gold ones.

FRIEND: But they're fake.

FIFTY: No. They're better. They have longer terms.

FRIEND: Where did you get them?

FIFTY: I can't tell you. I had them and I gave them to two little old women who gave me theirs in return.

FRIEND: They must have been really senile. No one would do that voluntarily.

FIFTY: I helped them along a bit.

FRIEND: You mean, you took them by force? Do you know what you are?

FIFTY: I don't care what I am. Everybody is something. So I've got to be something too. But I've got two lockets and I can do with them whatever I want.

FRIEND: I don't believe you. Why are you telling me this?

FIFTY: You can report me. If you're afraid, I give you permission to dissolve our friendship. I won't be mad with you. You're shaking.

FRIEND: Really, what should I be afraid of? I didn't do anything. But I feel guilty. I wish I'd never talked to you. *I* pushed you in this direction. I should never have answered your questions. I'm the one to blame. I am the criminal. And you tell me to report you!

FIFTY: Don't worry about it. Help me instead! Help me! It's done.

FRIEND: How can I help you? You know what you've become.

FIFTY: A murderer. A common thief and murderer. Or whatever it's called. But who cares what they call you. Help me open the lockets!

FRIEND: Help you open them! You want to open them!

FIFTY: I want to see what's in them. You know what's supposed to be in them.

FRIEND: But what good is that supposed to do? You know what you're going to find there.

FIFTY: Do I really?

FRIEND: Yes! Yes! Every child knows that. Everyone is carrying it on him all his life. You just know.

FIFTY: Have you ever seen one from inside?

FRIEND: No. But that's not necessary.

FIFTY: You've never seen one!

FRIEND: But I saw my father laid out. And before that I saw my . . . do I have to tell you again? You know how much her death still hurts me today. I was there. You understand! I was there. I was there when the coroner found the locket and opened it. I was there when he entered the death in the register.

FIFTY: But did you check the locket yourself?

FRIEND: No! You're asking too much of me. I was much too upset. I was in no state to look at numbers! But there were lots of other people. There were plenty of witnesses!

FIFTY: They were as upset as you. *Nobody* has seen the inside of her locket! Nobody! The only one who wasn't upset was the Locketeer. He's never upset. He's used to it. He's the one who sees it all and registers it all.

FRIEND: And you don't believe him because you hate him. I should have never sent you to him.

FIFTY: Come on now; I don't hate anybody! But I don't believe anybody. It's too important to me. I want to open those lockets myself and have a look with my own eyes. I'm going to open them. Believe me. No one's going to stop me. I want you to help me.

FRIEND: I want to help you. But how can I do that? How can I help? It's almost done.

FIFTY: I need your eyes. I want you to see *with me* what's inside those lockets. I don't trust my eyes. I am biased. And when I tell you what I've just found, you wouldn't believe me.

FRIEND: Now I understand. You want me to be there when you open them.

FIFTY: Exactly. Don't let me down now. You must understand what's at stake.

FRIEND: I don't understand what's at stake. Maybe I'll never understand.

FIFTY: But you won't let me down.

FRIEND: No. I won't let you down.

FIFTY: Here they are. How could we open them?

FRIEND: That's supposed to be very difficult. The Locketeer has a key.

FIFTY: We'll have to break them open.

FRIEND: I'm afraid so. It's the only way.

FIFTY: Do you have a hammer?

FRIEND: Here.

FIFTY: Thanks. I'm ready to hit.

FRIEND: But be careful. Careful. You mustn't damage what's in there.

FIFTY: (*Hits.*) Here we go!

FRIEND: Let me see! Is it open?

FIFTY: No. Just dented. Strange, the way they're made.

FRIEND: Now what?

FIFTY: I'm hitting once more. (*Hits.*) Now give me a file.

FRIEND: Here you go.

FIFTY: I think it'll work. Wait. Maybe you could hold it right here.

FRIEND: There. I am holding the chain.

FIFTY: I've got it! It's open! Open! Open! Take a look. You look first! What do you see?

FRIEND: Nothing.

FIFTY: Nothing. It's empty.

FRIEND: Empty. That must be a mistake. Where's the second one?

FIFTY: Here it is. Give me the hammer. (*He hits.*) The file. Now hold the chain! Tightly. There. (*He works with the file.*) It's open. This time I want to look first.

FRIEND: No. Let's do it together.

FIFTY: It's better to do it alone. Let me go first.

FRIEND: Whatever you think. What do you see?

FIFTY: Nothing. Nothing. It's empty.

FRIEND: What? This one too? . . . Yes. It's empty. What does that mean?

FIFTY: That's what I'm asking you.

FRIEND: The little old ladies have fooled you. They didn't give you their real lockets.

FIFTY: You think so? I don't. You weren't there. You would have had to be there.

FRIEND: But you can see for yourself that they are empty.

FIFTY: That's just it. The lockets *are* empty. Don't you understand?

FRIEND: Nonsense! You are crazy!

FIFTY: Here's mine. Give me yours. Let's open both!

FRIEND: I—I can't. Forgive me. I won't let you have mine. And I don't want you to open yours.

FIFTY: You can't prevent me. I don't need yours. Here's my locket. Hit it!

FRIEND: No.

FIFTY: Coward. Let me have the hammer.

FRIEND: I—I can't give it to you.

FIFTY: Then I'll just take it. I'm not afraid.

FRIEND: What are you doing! What are you doing!

FIFTY: You're like the old women. (*Hits.*) Now I've smashed it. Help me with the file.

FRIEND: I've got the chain.

FIFTY: It's open. It's open. My own locket is open! Take a look! I hereby pronounce you locketeer! What do you see?

FRIEND: (*Shaking.*) Nothing. It's empty.

FIFTY: Nothing. It's empty too. *All lockets are empty.*

FRIEND: That's not possible! Get out of here. Quick! You are playing a dirty game with me. You're no longer my friend. What's the point of your magic tricks with fake lockets which you supposedly steal and fake lockets which you put around you neck. You think that's funny. But it's very painful to me. I don't ever want to see you again. Do you think your ugly tricks will bring me back my sister! Go, I hate you! I hate you!

FIFTY: You don't believe me. Why don't you give me your own locket before you start accusing me. Did I fake yours and put it around your neck? Surely you must know your own locket! You make heavy accusations. Let me tell you: You are not only my best, you are my only friend. And you really think that I could be such a bastard. Let me have a chance to defend myself. Sacrifice your locket for me! You are standing right in front of me. You have it on you. You always had it on you. You haven't taken it off since the day you were born, not *once*! Not even once have you taken it off. I'll go way over to the other side of the room. I'll stay there. I won't move. You go ahead and open your own locket. You owe it to me! Do it! Do it!

FRIEND: I can't. I am afraid of you. What do you want from me? Leave me alone.

FIFTY: You don't want to have anything to do with me anymore.

FRIEND: I want you to leave me alone.

FIFTY: I am leaving. Farewell!

FRIEND: You are leaving. But how am I supposed to go on now?

FIFTY: I haven't done anything to you.

FRIEND: No. Nothing. Why don't you go now! Just go! Go!

FIFTY: I'm not angry with you. Farewell.

FRIEND: No. You're not angry with me. But I am angry with you! I hate you! Go!

FIFTY: What shall I do?

FRIEND: Nothing. Just go.

FIFTY: All right. Farewell.

FIFTY AND LOCKETEER

FIFTY: What about those who passed away too soon?

LOCKETEER: Nobody passed away too soon.

FIFTY: My friend had a sister who passed away at the age of twelve.

LOCKETEER: That was her legal name.

FIFTY: Legal! A law based on ignorance!

LOCKETEER: That's what all laws are about. There is only one thing that matters when it comes to laws and that is that they are being observed.

FIFTY: By everyone?

LOCKETEER: By everyone living under their jurisdiction.

FIFTY: What about those who had lived earlier?

LOCKETEER: They couldn't live accordingly. Do you have any more intelligent, urgent questions?

FIFTY: What would happen if people suddenly were to find out that all lockets are empty?

LOCKETEER: There is no way for them to find out. Who would tell them such utter nonsense, such a horrible thing?

FIFTY: Let's assume, there's someone who has the *crazy idea* that all lockets are empty. So he takes to the street like a barker or let's say a new Mohammed and instead of shouting: "God is great and Mohammed is his prophet!" he'd exclaim: "The lockets are empty and nobody knows! The lockets are empty! The lockets are empty and nobody knows!"

LOCKETEER: Nobody would believe him. He'd soon stop shouting.

FIFTY: What if he would empty a locket and run through the streets with the empty case?

LOCKETEER: We all know what happens to murderers.

FIFTY: But I am concerned. I am terribly concerned. Once it has been *proclaimed,* this idea could spread and take roots.

LOCKETEER: Your concern is a credit to you and it shall be remembered in the future. But generations of locketeers have thought about this and made the necessary arrangements. Not for nothing has the stigma of murder been attached to the theft of a locket. And as you can see it has proven effective up to now.

FIFTY: But I am thinking about the future.

LOCKETEER: You are thinking too much about the future . . . a carry-over from your rebellious period.

FIFTY: Does it worry you? Do you consider my obsession harmful?

LOCKETEER: I wouldn't say that. You are no longer a danger. You recanted in public. You are considered a coward and a fool. Even if you were to revert to your old doubts and proclaim them all over town again you couldn't impress a soul. Only the innocent are really believed. The apostate will succeed only in the service of his new faith while his old faith is lost to him to a far greater degree than he could ever imagine.

FIFTY: What makes you think that I could dissent again?

LOCKETEER: I don't think you will. I've only explained to you why you are no longer a danger.

FIFTY: But you disapprove of my fears?

LOCKETEER: There is knowledge which is harmless and there is knowledge that is dangerous. But even more dangerous are certain doubts. And you have been cured of those in any event.

FIFY: What do you mean by that?

LOCKETEER: Nothing in particular. There are certain doubts which can drive a person to madness and despair. And those doubts are worse than dangerous knowledge. Because knowledge can be kept to oneself.

FIFTY: I have frightened you. I shouldn't have said that the lockets might be empty.

LOCKETEER: You haven't frightened me in the least. You have opened your locket and found nothing in it. I have done it a thousand times. Do I look frightened?

FIFTY: You really believe that I could have done such a thing?

LOCKETEER: There isn't much to believe. Nobody, who hasn't done it, has ever had that kind of thought. You are a murderer. But murderers who recant in time are of no interest to us.

FIFTY: You are accusing me of murder without any proof.

LOCKETEER: I spare you the proof. It would be too easy. You can have your freedom. Now you also know that you will live as long . . . well, as long as you will live. That's the kind of freedom you were after. That's the freedom you have stolen. Now enjoy it to your heart's delight! You may rest assured that there are other fools like you, who prefer your kind of deadly uncertainty to the certainty which we have established and intend to maintain.

FIFTY: There really are others like me?

LOCKETEER: Let me assure you, you are not unique. In fact, you have found out yourself that you are nothing special the moment you were willing to recant for one more day of life. You are such a coward that you can't even admit to your cowardice. But now you'll be able to thoroughly enjoy your cowardice. Because instead of just *one moment* you will have nothing but such *moments* ahead of you. I wouldn't dream of having you arrested as a murderer. Enjoy your successful robbery. I leave you to your *fear*.

FIFTY IN THE STREETS, LIKE A BARKER, BUT ALSO TOTALLY OBSESSED

FIFTY: I don't want to have anything to do with any of you. I don't give a damn about you. I don't give a damn because you don't exist. You are not alive. You're all dead. I am the only one. I am alive. I don't know when I'm going to die, that's why I am the only one. You're dragging on, with this precious, tiny burden around your neck. You have your years wrapped around your neck. Are they weighing you down? No! They aren't heavy. They aren't many! But you don't mind. Because you're already dead! I can't even see you. You're not even shadows! You are nothing. The only reason for my being with you is to let you know how much I despise you. Listen, people, all you good dead people out there. Even the years you're carrying around your neck are a fraud. You think they are yours. You are so certain. But nothing is certain. It's a fraud. You are carrying empty lockets around your neck. You don't even get the years which you think you are getting! You've got nothing! Nothing is certain! The lockets are empty! Everything is as uncertain as it has always been. If you want to die you can do it today. And if you don't want to, well, you'll still have to! The lockets are empty! The lockets are empty.

THE YOUNG GENTLEMEN

FIRST YOUNG GENTLEMAN: Here comes our savior!

SECOND YOUNG GENTLEMAN: Our savior! Our savior!

FIRST: What has he actually done?

SECOND: He has looked inside the locket.

FIRST: I could have done that!

SECOND: So why didn't you?

FIRST: I never thought of it.

SECOND: There you are! It's not as easy as you think.

FIRST: Did you ever try?

SECOND: To tell you the truth, yes. But it's impossible to open the darn thing.

FIRST: So what did you do with it?

SECOND: I threw mine away, that's all.

FIRST: I didn't. I'd never.

SECOND: You think yours is so special?

FIRST: It's still possible that everything will change.

SECOND: What should be changing?

FIRST: I'm waiting for the Locketeer's comment.

SECOND: The Locketeer! That swindler!

FIRST: Aren't you a bit rash?

SECOND: No, but you are a bit slow! You've got to be a swindler to survive!

FIRST: Frankly, I don't like this sudden change.

SECOND: And why not? Why not?

FIRST: Have you given it some thought?

SECOND: What's there to think about? The lockets are empty.

FIRST: Did you examine every single locket?

SECOND: What are you trying to tell me?

FIRST: Maybe some are empty and others have something inside.

SECOND: You are hopeless! That would be an even bigger fraud!

FIRST: How can you talk like that? What's supposed to happen to us now?

SECOND: What's supposed to happen! What's supposed to happen? We are *free* now!

FIRST: What do you mean?

SECOND: I am no longer afraid that I'll have to die with Twenty-eight.

FIRST: I am afraid that I may die before Eighty-eight.

SECOND: Well, you've been privileged up to now. Now the time of reckoning has come for people like you.

FIRST: But why? Tell me, why? What have I done to you?

SECOND: What have you done to me? You were some kind of a God. Just because of your damned name! Why should you be called Eighty-eight and I Twenty-eight? Are you better than I? Are you smarter? Do you work harder? On the contrary. You're dumber, you're lazier, you've got much less to offer than I! But it always used to be: Look at Eighty-eight, well, that's Eighty-eight!

FIRST: I never noticed a thing.

SECOND: So you never noticed that all the girls were after you? Wherever you showed up, you immediately became the center of attention. You could have married any one of them. But you didn't have to marry any of them. The aura of your noble name was honor enough.

FIRST: But all this has always been a great nuisance to me. If you could've only known what a nuisance it was.

SECOND: No one ever noticed. You took it all very much in stride.

FIRST: What else was I supposed to do?

SECOND: You have used this fraud to your best advantage. Did it occur to you even *once* to look inside your locket?

FIRST: No, that never occurred to me. But what about you? Why didn't you look?

SECOND: Because I was afraid. Who wants to be a murderer?

FIRST: It was a good law. Everything was calm.

SECOND: And now you've lost your calm!

FIRST: Not only I! Everyone! Everyone did! How do you know that you won't drop dead within the hour?

SECOND: I don't know. But this is better, *fairer*, than before, because I know that you too could drop dead within the hour.

FIRST: So what's this to you?

SECOND: Everything!

FIRST: You're consumed by envy! I don't know envy.

SECOND: You'll soon find out about envy. Just have a little patience.

FIRST: What's going to happen to the Locketeer?

SECOND: He'll be tried and duly punished.

FIRST: They can't do that. How could they penalize him for doing his duty? He'll be acquitted.

SECOND: You bet he won't! Believe me. You're in for a few surprises! If the Locketeer gets acquitted there'll be a revolution.

FIRST: You are wrong there. Even the savior wants everything to happen without any bloodshed.

SECOND: Savior. It sounds strange coming out of your mouth! Deep down you hate him, don't you! You better watch what you say about him.

FIRST: I haven't said anything bad about him.

SECND: But I can feel it between your words: Your hate is obvious.

FIRST: Oh well, you just know everything better.

SECOND: No, but I'm fed up with you calling all the shots. I'm fed up! Fed up! Fed up!

FIRST: Who'd ever think that you're my own brother.

SECOND: Indeed. Who would have thought so, when they called you Eighty-eight and me Twenty-eight!

TWO COLLEAGUES

FIRST COLLEAGUE: Now it seems that people weren't content after all.

SECOND COLLEAGUE: So much hate had been building up.

FIRST: Who would have thought so! People are going wild! I've just witnessed a scene which I will never forget.

SECOND: Tell me.

FIRST: There are masses of people, the streets were packed with people, and suddenly one of them is lifted up on another's shoulders, and he screams at the top of his lungs: "No more lockets! We don't need that stuff!" He tears open his shirt, pulls off his locket and throws it to the people. The masses cheer. Some follow his example, men first, then women, they rip through their shirts and throw off their lockets. "No more lockets." Someone jumps up and shouts: "Life to the people! Life to the people! Now we can live as long as we want to! Freedom! Freedom!''—And the masses shout back: "As long as we want! Freedom! Freedom!'' I got carried away too. I followed the crowd. It was as if someone guided my hand to my chest. I pulled off the thing and threw it up in the air. "So long lockets! We won't die!'' And the raging crowd picks up my cheer and everyone is screaming: "We won't die! We won't die!''

SECOND: But what's that supposed to mean? It doesn't mean a thing.

FIRST: It means, what it means. Everybody's sick of dying. Aren't you sick of it?

SECOND: Yes.

FIRST: So what do you want? What are you complaining about? What's your point? The people have rediscovered their right to live.

SECOND: So from now on everyone's going to decide for himself how long he's going to live?

FIRST: There won't be much to decide. Everyone's going to live forever.

SECOND: Everyone's going to live forever. Sounds wonderful.

FIRST: Not only does it sound wonderful, it *is* wonderful!

SECOND: But is it true?

FIRST: You love being the skeptic. I bet you've still got it, your locket. You'd rather be cautious, right? You'd rather hold on to what you have, don't you? You'd rather not take any risks? You are some hero! Have you got it? Yes or no?

SECOND: That's none of your business.

FIRST: It is very much my business.

SECOND: I can do with my locket whatever I please.

FIRST: You think so? That's what you think! Give it to me! Right now! It must be destroyed.

SECOND: No! I won't give it to you! I am keeping my locket.

FIRST: The hell you will! Give it to me! Now! (*He starts to strangle him.*)

SECOND: Help! He's killing me! He's taking my locket! Murder! Murder!

FIRST: Idiot! That's no longer a murder! Give me your locket or there will be a murder!

SECOND: (*Trembling.*) You take it. I'll keep still! You'll regret it some day!

FIRST: Regret? Dummy! When? Why? There's that empty little fake! Step on it!

SECOND: I can't.

FIRST: Step on it or I'll kill you!

SECOND: (*Shaking all over, he steps on it and then drops dead.*)

LOCKETEER AND FIFTY

FIFTY: But where will it end?

LOCKETEER: There won't be an end. Everything is shaken to the core.

FIFTY: I shouldn't have started.

LOCKETEER: It's too late now.

FIFTY: I've done it. Is there nothing I can do now to stop this tragedy?

LOCKETEER: Every murderer has asked this question, but only when it was too late.

FIFTY: What if I set a good example? What if I'd get up again in front of everybody and admit to my crime, bravely and honestly, and this time really honestly? What if I warn them and then, to prove the seriousness of my warning, drop dead in front of them? Is there nothing I can do to convince them? Nothing that could be useful to all of them? There may come others some other day who try to do what I did, and fail and bring confusion into the world. I am so ashamed. Most of all, I am ashamed for my blindness.

LOCKETEER: It's too late. Too late. I'm afraid, you have achieved what you set out to do.

FIFTY: You think that everybody knows now?

LOCKETEER: You have picked a terrific tune. Everybody's picked it up. I wouldn't have thought that they'd catch on that quickly and that well.

FIFTY: You've underestimated me. It's all your fault!

LOCKETEER: You really believe this?

FIFTY: You have been appointed as the guardian. You had been sworn into a high and noble office. And you knew very well, *what* it was you were guarding. You have treated me with arrogance and superiority. You should have destroyed me right away. How could you underestimate me so? With all your experience!

LOCKETEER: All my experience came from the dead.

FIFTY: You were only interested in your corpses. In the pomp and vanity of your office. Didn't you have plenty of opportunities to observe people who were still *alive*? The relatives of the dead? Were your ceremonies always in control, solemn and beyond any doubt? Was there never a time when something happened? Something unexpected? Did that never happen?

LOCKETEER: No. Nothing ever happened.

FIFTY: What kind of people did you live among?

LOCKETEER: Among content people. They were people who were no longer afraid.

FIFTY: There wasn't much left to learn then, was there?

FIFTY AND FRIEND

FRIEND: Is it you?

FIFTY: Yes. Don't you recognize me?

FRIEND: I don't recognize anyone with certainty anymore.

FIFTY: What's wrong? What happened?

FRIEND: I am looking for my sister.

FIFTY: How could you be looking for her?

FRIEND: She went into hiding.

FIFTY: Into hiding? Are you sure?

FRIEND: She went into hiding and I don't know where. I have been looking everywhere.

FIFTY: But how can you be so sure?

FRIEND: I know it. I know it.

FIFTY: But why would she have gone into hiding?

FRIEND: She was afraid.

FIFTY: Afraid of what?

FRIEND: She was afraid of her name. She was told that she had to die with Twelve. Those bastards were after her and they terrified her. She was living for years with this fear and she became increasingly quiet. We didn't know why she was talking so little, we had no idea. But then, on her birthday, her fear took over and she disappeared. She went to where people didn't know her name. She was afraid of her name. She has been hiding ever since. No one in my family has ever seen her again. She has avoided us like the plague. But we are looking for her everywhere. Actually, it's only me who is really looking for her. That's all I am doing these days and I know that I will find her.

FIFTY: But why do you want to upset her? Let her have her new life. She's much better off without you charging into her life. Her fear must have been tremendous, otherwise she wouldn't have been hiding for so long. If I'm not mistaken, it's been over thirty years.

FRIEND: That's just it. That's why it is so difficult to find her. Sometimes I think that I won't recognize her anymore. But I only have those thoughts when I am weary and drained from my search and overcome by hopelessness. That's when I usually fall asleep and as soon as I wake up, rested and refreshed, I have no doubt that I will recognize her, immediately from any distance, even if it were thirty years from now. Just let her come toward me and I'll touch her arm lightly, very softly, as if I wanted to caress her, but not like a stranger, no, this way, you see . . . and I would tell her that it is me.

FIFTY: She would think that you came to arrest her.

FRIEND: (*Angrily.*) Me? Arrest her? My little sister! How can you say that? You've lost your mind.

FIFTY: Please understand me! Of course you don't want to arrest her! Of course you want only the best and all the love in the world for her. But if she had left in terror of her name, she must believe that she had done something wrong. She is avoiding you in order to avoid punishment.

FRIEND: She hasn't done anything wrong. She was afraid and rightly so. She was a child and the stupid talk of the people around her frightened her.

FIFTY: Exactly. So she has started a new life. She keeps away from all of you, because she assumes that you would drag her back into her old life. She can only feel safe, that is to say unrecognized, among new faces.

FRIEND: I want to tell her the truth. I want to tell her that her name means nothing. I want to take her fear away from her. Then she'll return to us.

FIFTY: But don't you see that she already has a new name? She must have taken a new name. Otherwise her escape wouldn't have made any sense.

FRIEND: She'll tell me all about it. She'll tell me her new name.

FIFTY: And what will you call her?

FRIEND: To me, she'll always be my little sister. She hasn't changed. She is what she's always been. My dearest little sister. The dearest person in the world.

FIFTY: But thirty years older.

FRIEND: Nonsense! That's what you think. She hasn't aged at all.

FIFTY: I'm not saying that she has aged. But she is thirty years older and she must have changed.

FRIEND: I don't believe it.

FIFTY: Don't be so stubborn. She is now forty-two years old. How can she look like a child of twelve?

FRIEND: To me she is twelve.

FIFTY: And you'll call her by her name?

FRIEND: Of course. What else! Twelve, Twelve, that's what I'll say and I'll take her in my arms and pull her by her hair the way I used to, and I'll shake her and rock her and hold her out the window, until she'll beg me to let go of her! Twelve, Twelve, I'll say, don't you see that it's all nonsense, all names are nonsense, it makes no difference what one is called, whether it's Twelve or Eighty-eight or the devil knows what! As long as we are here, together, and we see each other and we talk to each other. Twelve, can you hear me, Twelve, can you see me, Twelve, it's me, Twelve, it'll always be me.

FIFTY: But what about her? What about her? What makes you think that she'll be as happy as you? Perhaps she is happier now. Perhaps she didn't like it among you.

FRIEND: Perhaps! Perhaps! Perhaps! I *know* what I am talking about. There's no perhaps for me!

FIFTY: Why don't you let her live *the way she wants to*. You want to force her to return. That's not right. It isn't fair. You don't really love her. If you did, you'd be doing everything the way *she* wants it. If you're not just talking, you must let go of her.

FRIEND: I am not just talking. That's why I'm looking for her. That's why I shall find her.

END

Gitta Honegger was a member of the Vienna Burgtheater, the Schauspielhaus Zurich, and other German repertory companies, before coming to the U.S. She has worked at the Guthrie, Long Wharf, La Mama, Public Theater, Ensemble Studio Theater and, most recently, at Arena Stage. Her translation of plays by Austrian writer Thomas Bernhard, *The President and Eve of Retirement,* was published by Performing Arts Journal Publications.

Klaus Völker has worked as a dramaturg at theatres in Zurich, Basel, and Bremen, and since 1980 at the Schiller Theatre in Berlin. He is the author of *Brecht Chronicle* and *Bertolt Brecht: A Biography,* and co-editor of the collected works of Brecht in German.

PAJ PLAYSCRIPT SERIES

General Editors: Bonnie Marranca and Gautam Dasgupta

OTHER TITLES IN THE SERIES:

THEATRE OF THE RIDICULOUS/Kenneth Bernard, Charles Ludlam, Ronald Tavel

ANIMATIONS: A TRILOGY FOR MABOU MINES/Lee Breuer

THE RED ROBINS/Kenneth Koch

THE WOMEN'S PROJECT/Penelope Gilliatt, Lavonne Mueller, Rose Leiman Goldemberg, Joyce Aaron-Luna Tarlo, Kathleen Collins, Joan Schenkar, Phyllis Purscell

WORDPLAYS: NEW AMERICAN DRAMA/Maria Irene Fornes, Ronald Tavel, Jean-Claude van Itallie, Richard Nelson, William Hauptman, John Wellman

BEELZEBUB SONATA/Stanislaw I. Witkiewicz

DIVISION STREET AND OTHER PLAYS/Steve Tesich

TABLE SETTINGS/James Lapine

THE PRESIDENT AND EVE OF RETIREMENT/Thomas Bernhard

TWELVE DREAMS/James Lapine

SICILIAN COMEDIES/Luigi Pirandello

WORDPLAYS 2: NEW AMERICAN DRAMA/Rochelle Owens, Wallace Shawn, Len Jenkin, Harry Kondoleon, John O'Keefe

THE ENTHUSIASTS/Robert Musil